STONE'S RULES

STONE'S RULES

How to Win at Politics, Business, and Style

ROGER STONE

INTRODUCTION BY TUCKER CARLSON
EDITED BY TYLER PATRICK NIXON

CURATED BY KEVIN RYAN

Skyhorse Publishing

Skyhorse Publishing books may be purchased in bulk at special discounts for sales promotion, corporate gifts, fund-raising, or educational purposes. Special editions can also be created to specifications. For details, contact the Special Sales Department, Skyhorse Publishing, 307 West 36th Street, 11th Floor, New York, NY 10018 or info@skyhorsepublishing.com.

Skyhorse® and Skyhorse Publishing® are registered trademarks of Skyhorse Publishing, Inc.®, a Delaware corporation.

Visit our website at www.skyhorsepublishing.com.

10 9 8 7 6 5 4 3 2 1

Library of Congress Cataloging-in-Publication Data is available on file.

Cover design by Brian Peterson
Cover photo credit *Business Insider*

ISBN: 978-1-5107-4008-2
Ebook ISBN: 978-1-5107-4009-9

Printed in the United States of America

To Nydia Bertran Stone: my life's partner who has suffered my enthusiasms, shared my victories, and given solace in my defeats.

"It is not the critic who counts; not the man who points out how the strong man stumbles or where the doer of deeds could have done them better. The credit belongs to the man who is actually in the arena, whose face is marred by dust and sweat and blood; who strives valiantly; who errs, and comes short again and again; because there is not effort without error and shortcoming; but who does actually strive to do the deeds; who knows the great enthusiasms, the devotions; who spends himself in a worthy cause, who at the best knows in the end the triumphs of high achievement and who at worst, if he fails, at least fails while daring greatly, so that his place shall never be with those cold and timid souls who know neither victory or defeat."

—*Theodore Roosevelt*

CONTENTS

INTRODUCTION

By Tucker Carlson

People often accuse the media of having an agenda, and in some ways they're right. Most journalists are conventional liberals, and the coverage often reflects that. But outright manipulation of content? I've rarely seen it. In fact, in more than two decades of working in the news and opinion business, I can think of only a single time I've been censored outright. It was the day a network executive forbade me to interview the author of this book.

"Just so you know," he said, "the problem isn't that Roger Stone is conservative. We have conservatives on all the time." OK, I said, then what is the problem? Well, the executive conceded, Stone does know everything about politics. And he is famous. And articulate. And entertaining. But you still can't have him on.

Huh?

It was obvious I was never going to get a straight answer, mostly because there wasn't one. The executive obviously liked and respected Roger—he told me so in hushed tones—but for reasons he couldn't quite articulate, he worried that booking him would somehow bring trouble to the network. Like many in the upper reaches of media, business and government, this executive stood in fear and trembling before the legend of Roger Stone.

And for good reason: Roger Stone is a troublemaker—indeed, not just a troublemaker, but perhaps the premier troublemaker of our time, the Michael Jordan of electoral mischief. This is either terrifying or delightful, depending on your uptightness level. I love it. Television executives don't. That's the difference.

But Roger Stone is more that just the most colorful political operative in America, a man who for thirty years has blurred the line between high-level consulting and performance art. He is also wise, as you'll learn in the following pages.

From his early years with Richard Nixon, to his work subverting democracy during the 2000 Florida recount, Roger has been paying keen attention to the human drama and drawing lessons from it. Psychology, business, power, partisanship, food, fashion—he has deep insights into all of it, and equally deep convictions.

Cufflinks should be small, betrayals should be avenged, and political debts should be paid. And under no circumstances should your pocket square ever match your necktie, on pain of death. That's Roger's advice, or the beginning of it.

If you've been to the self-help section of your local bookstore lately, you know there are almost as many guides to life as there are people looking for guidance in life. Yet, crack the cover of any of them and you'll recognize the same recurring themes: stop struggling; accept yourself; be who you are. Robert Fulgham, Rick Warren, and Deepak Chopra may come from three distinct religious traditions, but all wind up at the same destination, floating peacefully in the soothing waters of Lake Me.

Not Roger. His counsel is earthier, more outwardly focused, and probably more honest. Here, for example, is Roger on forgiveness: "I will often wait years to take my revenge, hiding in the tall grass, my stiletto at the ready, waiting patiently until you think I have forgotten or forgiven a past slight and then, when you least expect it, I will spring from the underbrush and plunge a dagger up under your ribcage."

It turns out that everything you needed to know was not covered in kindergarten.

I could go on, from memory, but you've got rules to read. Roger and I disagree on pleated trousers, but other than that, he's on the level. Enjoy.

—*Tucker Carlson*

PREFACE

For thirty years I have been on the front line of American presidential politics, serving eight national Republican presidential candidates. I have engineered the elections of senators and governors.

In the business world, I have assisted multi-billion-dollar mergers and acquisitions. I have solved complex public relations and political problems for corporations, pro-Western foreign governments, trade associations, and wealthy individuals.

Over my many years as a consummate political animal I:

Spent untold hours talking politics and learning political tactics from Richard Nixon, whose presence on six presidential ballots nationwide is surpassed only by Franklin Roosevelt;

Served as a traveling aide for the great American patriot, Senator Bob Dole—driving him while he was in Washington D.C, cutting up his meat, and occasionally helping him with a collar button (Dole's courage and persistence allowed him to overcome the grave battlefield injuries he suffered when hit by a German shell in Italy);

Regularly briefed and prepped Ronald Reagan while organizing his Presidential campaigns in 1976, 1980, and 1984;

Targeted ethnic Catholic Democrats for the election of Ronald Reagan in 1980 and 1984;

Was sent on a mission in 1988 by James Baker that allowed George H. W. Bush to beat Mike Dukakis in California by *one point*.

My efforts resulted in toppling corrupt New York Governor Eliot Spitzer, who was using the services of multiple call girl rings while prosecuting others for prostitution. Spitzer funded his early political career with an illegal loan from his billionaire father and then perjured himself in a civil suit filed by his disgruntled Democratic primary competitors.

I helped undermine the Reform Party after they cost Republicans the White House in 1988. I shut down the 2000 Florida presidential recount in Miami-Dade County by fomenting a riot, and I launched the idea of Donald J. Trump for President.

My nearly four decades in the political arena have made me an extraordinary cast of enemies. I've been attacked by David Byrne of Talking Heads, Rosie O'Donnell, washed-up clown Tom Arnold, fantasy novelist J.K. Rowling, unemployable lunatic Keith Olbermann, a bevy of elitist twits at the *Daily Beast*, knife-in-the-back propagandists at *HuffPo*, and a chorus of other fake news sites like *Raw Story* and *Salon* and *Slate* and the dipshits at *Mother Jones*, which endlessly spew assorted and sundry bullshit about yours truly.

I have been able to make Ari Melber, the hapless dope at MSNBC, sputter, and the brainless talking heads at CNN like Jake Tapper and Ana Navarro rage. I love it. As I said in the culmination of the Netflix documentary *Get Me Roger Stone*, "I revel in their hatred because if I was not effective, they would not hate me."

My favorite quote from the Joker, the villain in the Batman comics, is, "Introduce a little anarchy. Upset the established order, and everything becomes chaos. I'm an agent of chaos. Oh, and you know the thing about chaos? It's fair!"

I will admit I love ruffling the feathers of the Democrat-GOP ruling duopoly and the elites of both parties, who have worked in tandem to drive America into a ditch. The Bushes and Clintons and Obamas have seamlessly colluded to promulgate and perpetuate policies that have uniformly made America weaker and have bankrupted us, while they and their crony corporatist friends have enriched themselves by exploiting the system they have corrupted in such cynical fashion over decades.

In 2012, I even had to bolt from my longtime political home, the party of Lincoln and Goldwater, in revulsion over its nomination of Mitt Romney, whose father Michigan Governor George Romney stabbed Barry Goldwater in the back in 1964. Mitt Romney is not a conservative and only became a Republican after deciding to run for governor of Massachusetts. In 1980, Mitt supported Massachusetts liberal Paul Tsongas over Ronald Reagan.

I had great sentimental attachment to the Republican Party, having served as young Republican National Chairman from 1977 to 1979 and having worked for the campaigns of four Republican presidential nominees. During that brief stint in which I left the GOP over the Romney nomination debacle, I proudly supported the presidential ticket of Governor Gary Johnson and his running mate Judge Jim Gray.

Johnson was a successful New Mexico governor who cut taxes and regulations and spending, while advocating the legalization of marijuana and same-sex marriage. With Donald Trump's hostile takeover of the Republican Party in 2016, I returned to the GOP, comfortable again battling the country club Republicans.

My decades of provocative, unconventional, often-wild forays into American politics have also garnered me some outlandish monikers in the media . . .

The *Weekly Standard* anointed me the "High Priest of Political Mischief."

L.A. Weekly (clearly aiming for neutral journalistic objectivity) described me as a "slash-and-burn Republican black bag election tamperer."

The *New York Times* credited me with "a long history of bare-knuckle politics."

The *Atlantic* called me "skilled in the dark arts of politics."

Politics1.com crowned me "the Jedi Master of the negative campaign."

The once-dominant, now-doddering ex-anchor from NBC News, Tom Brokaw, accused me of bringing "some kind of a James Bond evil factor in all of this."

Whether you think these are compliments or condemnation depends on your political point of view. One man's devil is another man's savior. One man's dirty trick is another man's civic participation. One man's dirty trickster is another man's freedom fighter.

To me, it all comes down to WINNING. It comes down to using any and every legal means available to achieve victory for my friends and allies, and to inflict crushing, ignominious defeat on my opponents and, yes, enemies.

Politics ain't beanbag; it is not for the faint of heart, nor is it a place where the risk-averse will ever find shelter. What sets me apart from the cookie-cutter crowd of conventional political consultants, strategists, and hired guns is that I never pretend otherwise. Political games are for others to play—I wage political warfare.

Some have called me a strategic genius and a master dirty trickster. I've been blamed for stealing the 2000 election for George W. Bush in Florida. I've been accused of destroying the National Reform Party after eccentric billionaire H. Ross Perot cost the GOP the White House in 1992 and 1996. I've been credited with propping up the candidacy of Reverend Al Sharpton to divide the Democrats in 2004.

It has even been suggested that I was behind the forging of Texas Air National Guard documents purportedly lifted from George W. Bush's service record that, on the eve of the 2004 general election, were fed to Dan Rather at CBS, ultimately destroying (by his own hand) Rather's career as one of America's top three network news anchors.

Those who claim I elected Trump are wrong. Trump elected Trump—he's persistent, driven to succeed, clever, stubborn, and deeply patriotic. I am, however, among a handful who saw his potential for national leadership and the presidency. The others were two former presidents. Both Reagan in the White House and in Nixon in his post-presidency make note of it.

As a lifelong witness, participant, and practicing patriot in our American political tradition, I have "made my bones" . . . and then some.

I have acquired many valuable lessons beginning from my first days as an ambitious 19-year-old upstart in the Nixon White House to my daily mission today waging pitched battle, almost around the clock, on every conceivable front, with every available resource, against a determined, well-funded, incredibly underhanded juggernaut of the dirtiest of dirty tricksters who are intent on subverting everything great about this country.

To those who accuse me of puffery and air-brushing myself into history, I will only plead guilty to being a "showman." If you cannot not be interesting, you cannot get anyone's attention. "Back-channel, intermediary, confirming source"—all the same thing. Dramatization is not exaggeration.

These lessons, garnered from nearly a half-century of intense political engagement, have translated into a collection of operating "rules," useful to anyone with ambition in life. This book is a collection of the best of all I have learned through decades at the top of American politics and business.

But *Stone's Rules* is not a political primer. It is a compendium of rules for war, politics, food, fashion, and life itself. It also includes my thoughts on advertising, public relations, and media.

Among other things, you will learn how much "linen" to show at the end of your suit cuff, a proper recipe for Sunday Gravy (the name real Italian Americans give to red sauce), how to design a billboard, how to select cufflinks, how to budget a political campaign, what to wear, and what *not* to wear, ever.

Think of *Stone's Rules* as the style manual for a "master of the universe"—the instruction book for someone who wants to move like a pro.

My many colleagues in the political world have been hearing me spout these maxims for decades. Now I share them with you.

—Roger J. Stone, Jr.
New York City
April 20, 2018

Photo credit Getty images

STONE'S RULES

PART #1

ENTERING THE ARENA

The original phrase, "There are men of action and men of thought," gives value to thinkers and philosophers, apart from men of deeds.

Thinking is great, and it is critical to conceiving and planning action. But ultimately it is action that determines the course and direction of civilization.

Leaders who are frozen in contemplation and indecision, those unwilling to take political risks, will ultimately lose.

As Theodore Roosevelt said, "the credit belongs to the man who is actually in the arena," not to those who stand on the sidelines and point out the failures and shortcomings of the man in the arena.

There is no political reward without risk. There is no shame in losing. There is only shame in failing to strive, in never trying at all.

YOU CAN'T WIN IF YOU DON'T GET IN THE GAME.

More precisely, you can't win if you don't run. I have seen veteran Congressmen with a solid political base wait around for the "right race" for governor or senator, ending up spending decades in the lower house.

Matt Rinaldo was a veteran Congressman from New Jersey. A moderate Republican, he was popular with Democrats and enjoyed union support. Potentially a strong statewide candidate, Rinaldo looked at every US Senate and gubernatorial race with interest—but never ran.

Rinaldo was a good man who did many good things for people in House of Representatives. He was a good politician who worked hard for his district. The polyester-clad man of the people could have done great things as governor or in the US Senate. I often think about Rinaldo's potential, lost to the ages because he waited and waited for the "right" moment . . . for that favorable race that never came.

Politics is about taking risks. You can't win if you don't run.

STONE'S RULE #3

DON'T HIDE YOUR SCARS, THEY MAKE YOU WHO YOU ARE . . . BUT DON'T FIGHT THE LAST WAR, EITHER.

Life is a battle. The lot of a political consultant is both seasonal and cyclical. I have experienced periods of great prosperity and periods of being dead broke. No two campaigns are alike, and the great mistake of many in my trade is the tendency to "fight the last war."

Democratic pros who ran Hillary Clinton's 2016 campaign simply assumed that black voters would support and turn-out for Hillary Clinton in comparable numbers to what Barack Obama had garnered. Their fatal miscalculation here is a classic example of fighting the last war.

Widespread awareness about Danney Williams, Bill Clinton's African American son who Bill had abandoned and Hillary had banished, was a trend among internet savvy African Americans that the Clinton campaign never spotted. No less than 38 million people saw conservative filmmaker Joel Gilbert's documentary *Banished: The Untold Story of Bill*

Clinton's Black Son, and at least 22 million people saw the catchy rap video by The Freenauts which told the Danney Williams story on multiple platforms, including the hip-hop media titan World-Star.

Donald Trump would eventually succeed in besting the vote totals of either Mitt Romney or John McCain in black precincts of Detroit, Milwaukee, Philadelphia, Charlotte, Richmond, Cleveland, and Miami-Fort Lauderdale. In every one of these cities, Hillary ran anywhere from three to seven points behind Barack Obama's high-water mark. In other words, African American voters elected Donald Trump.

As the years following November 2016 more than demonstrated, Hillary Clinton is perpetually mired in a dysfunctional obsession with fighting the last war, which saw her defeated in the most humiliating (and well-deserved) fashion imaginable. Hillary clearly fails to recognize that she is not only fighting the "last" war (as in the previous war), but that this war was also HER last war . . . the ignominious finale to her dubious, ultimately failed political career.

STONE'S RULE #4

PAST IS *FUCKING* PROLOGUE.

I'm constantly surprised by young reporters and political consultants who have no sense of history and precedent. To understand the future, you must study the past.

When I was among a select group trying to get Congressman Jack Kemp on the ticket with Ronald Reagan in 1980, I tipped the late Niles Lathem of the *New York Post* that powerful New York State Party Chairman Dick Rosenbaum, Nelson Rockefeller's ball buster, had told Reagan that Kemp was OK for VP.

"Rosenbaum gave 'em the signal," I said.

"Wow, that's big," said Lathem. "Who's Rosenbaum?"

Having instant, constant access to information is not the same as having knowledge or context for it. Trite as it may be, it is no less true, to paraphrase George Santayana, that those who ignore history are doomed to repeat it.

RULE

MAKE YOUR LUCK.

#5

Frank Sinatra, the Chairman of the Board, said it best: "People often remark that I'm pretty lucky. Luck is only important insofar as getting the chance to sell yourself at the right moment. After that, you've got to have talent and know how to use it."

Donald Trump is another success story whose life seems to have been blessed with luck, but Trump is a firm believer and practitioner of the rule that you must "make your luck," in his case through deft positioning and relentless drive.

STONE'S RULE #6

REACH HIGHER.

Abraham Lincoln lost races for the Illinois legislature, House, and two bids for the Senate before he eventually won the White House.

In 1957, New Jersey Congressman Harrison "Pete" Williams lost his House seat. Two years later, Williams ran for the Senate and won, serving in the Senate from 1959 to 1982. He would have served as long as he liked had he not been caught up in the Abscam scandal.

Bush *pater familia* Prescott Bush lost a Senate race in Connecticut after being tied to Planned Parenthood, in an effective bid by his opponent to deny Catholic votes to Bush. Two years later, Bush won a special election to fill a vacant Senate seat. Prior to his bids for Senate, Bush had never served in a position higher than moderator of the Greenwich Town Meeting.

My friend, the late senator from Pennsylvania, Arlen Specter, lost races for district attorney, governor, and Senator before finally snagging a Senate seat in 1980. Arlen never gave up.

New York's Alfonse D'Amato, a crude but effective pol, was the Hempstead Town Supervisor before he toppled the inestimable Jacob Javits in 1980, seizing the Senate seat Javits had held since 1957. Al had levied charges of poor health and infirmity against Javits—a political mugging.

In 2016, Donald Trump became the most improbable winner of the presidency perhaps in modern times. Against seemingly insurmountable odds, he out-thought, out-foxed, out-worked, out-messaged, and out-campaigned the sluggish, entitled political animal Hillary Rodham Clinton.

Dream big. Reach big. Try the impossible, because sometimes it works.

This story was told to me by the comedian John Byner, who heard it from an old black musician who toured with jazz great Louis Armstrong. I confirmed the anecdote with Charles McWhorter, who served as a traveling aide to then-Vice President Richard Nixon.

In the late 1950s, the State Department made Louis Armstrong an international "Goodwill Ambassador" and underwrote a series of concert tours through Europe and Asia.

On return from the first two tours, Satchmo and his entourage were waved through Customs without having their bags and belongings searched, thanks to his ambassadorial status.

In 1958, after his third tour, Armstrong landed at New York's Idlewild Airport, except this time he was directed to the usual Customs line for a thorough search. Customs agents had gotten a specific tip about contraband being smuggled into the country and were searching everyone entering the US, no exceptions.

Armstrong joined the long line of travelers waiting their turn for Customs agents to scrutinize their possessions. The problem was that among the world-famous trumpeter's possessions were three pounds of marijuana, right in his suitcase, apparently some of the goodwill returned to him in kind . . . the real kind.

Armstrong began sweating profusely, realizing he was about to get busted for trafficking narcotics into the country while traveling on behalf of the government. Aside from the penalties a black man would likely face for such an offense in America of 1958, jazz legend or not, Satchmo realized the shame it would bring to the country given his ambassadorial status, official or not. It's probably a safe bet Louis began praying mightily.

Within minutes, a set of doors swung open and into the Customs area swept none other than the Vice President of United States, Richard M. Nixon, buffered by his small security detail and followed by a gaggle of reporters and photographers.

Nixon spotted Satchmo, who also had drawn a small gaggle of people around him, waiting in the line and, ever the shrewd politician, saw an opportunity to get a wire photo with the beloved entertainer.

The Vice President diverted his entourage over to the jazz man and asked, "Satchmo, what are you doing here?"

"Well, Pops," (Armstrong called everyone Pops) "I just came back from my goodwill tour of Asia and they told me I had to stand in this line for Customs."

After some chit-chat (long enough for a photo to get snapped), Nixon, no stranger to physical labor, grabbed both of Satchmo's suitcases and said, "Ambassadors don't have to go through Customs and the Vice President of the United States will carry your bags to the exit. Do you have a car waiting?"

Whereupon, Richard Milhous Nixon, who just a decade later became the 37th President of the United States, "muled" three pounds of high-grade pot through Customs without ever knowing a thing about it.

Miracles do happen.

RULE

#8

IF LIFE IS A PERFORMANCE, BE A COSTUME.

The key to being a great dresser is to think carefully about it but make it look effortless and natural—*sprezzatura*, as the Italians call it. Think through what you will wear for your most important meetings and particularly on TV. Stick with basics and classics. No plaid sports jackets on TV unless you want to look like Rodney Danger-field in *Caddy Shack*.

A solid navy blue tie with a crisp white shirt, French blue shirt, or blue and white striped shirt is a sure winner when matched with a navy, charcoal grey, or pinstriped suit in blue or grey, single- or double-breasted. No blends. 100 percent wool or cotton; natural fibers only.

I once went to a New Jersey State Republican Convention in the 1970s, where there was so much double knit it was a fire-hazard.

Think through your leisure wear and eschew Lycra and synthetic fibers. Track suits are for pimps. Polo shirts, khakis, well cut jeans, pleated cotton shorts, and non-baggy T-shirts are tolerable, depending on climate.

Dress like a preppy even if you aren't one.

DEVELOP GOOD DRESSING HABITS EARLY.

Plain and simple as the dress is, it is a sure test of a gentlemanly appearance. The man who dresses for dinner every night of his life looks easy and natural in it, whereas the man who takes to it later in life generally succeeds in looking like a waiter.

STONE'S RULE #9

DRESS WITH SPREZZATURA.

A gentleman must show a graceful, easy carelessness. Never reveal calculation or effort. The appearance of exertion detracts from your look of nonchalance.

Fred Astaire used to throw a new suit or hat against the wall several times to get the "newness" out of it. Clothing must move with you creating an air of comfort and casualness. A look that is studied or carefully coordinated will look like a contrivance, detracting from your allure.

Think Gianni Agnelli, Cary Grant, Douglas Fairbanks Jr., William Powell, Ronald Coleman, Jack Buchanan, and Jack Kennedy—they all had *sprezzatura*. Jude Law, Jay-Z, Calvin Klein, and Lapo Elkann have it today. Even Fran Lebowitz, who has men's suits custom made for her by Anderson and Sheppard, has it. You can have it too.

DRESS BRITISH, THINK YIDDISH.

I first heard this from Reagan's Secretary of Labor, Ray Donovan, who was referring to his lawyers during the corruption investigation that forced him from the Cabinet.

English tailoring, with its soft shoulders and natural drape, emphasizes the power and shape of the upper body. Much of Savile Row tailoring comes from the military tradition that includes a full chest and tapered waist. Italian tailoring is softer and slouchier—ideal for nightclubs and card games but wrong for business meetings and legal conferences.

Thinking Yiddish is meant here as a compliment—meaning wise, canny, wily, and successfully.

Lyndon Johnson was a crude and vicious political competitor who viewed every contest he ran for public office as having the potential to end his life. Johnson ran aggressive campaigns and never put his eggs in one basket. When Johnson told a young aide, "To win you must do everything." The young man said, "Yes, sir."

"No," said Senator Johnson. "I mean everything . . ."

Indeed, Johnson meant everything, including murder. John F. Kennedy was the only thing that stood between LBJ and the top job in the land, for which he had lusted his entire life.

It is no small coincidence that when President Kennedy, on the eve of launching his 1964 reelection campaign, agreed to take a late fall political trip in 1963 to Johnson's home turf of Texas at the behest of LBJ's closest political friend and crony, Governor John Connally, Kennedy returned in a body bag and Johnson returned as president.

THINK BIG.
BE BIG.

These have been the watchwords of President Donald J. Trump, since long before he was elected. Trump made billions, lost them in the real estate crash, and got them all back. And won an "unwinnable" campaign against an "unbeatable" opponent.

Through it all, he never lost his optimism, his determination, or his confidence.

'**ve seen it all. From Watergate to the triumph of Reagan, the HUD scandal, the 2000 recount, the Bush crime family, the collapse of the neocons, the Clintons' war on women, the improbable rise of Donald Trump, and the continuing efforts by the deep state to destabilize and delegitimize his presidency,

Life is a battle and no matter how difficult the situation or how overwhelming the odds, one must never quit.

Winston Churchill, a man whose name is nearly synonymous with the word indefatigable, could not have said this more clearly than when he rallied the United Kingdom to persevere against the Nazis—to the bitter end, if necessary—saying, "Never, never, never give up!"

So, too, did Richard Nixon recognize this imperative. Nixon said, "A man is not finished when he is defeated, he is only finished when he quits."

If I don't get at least five death threats a week I figure I must be doing something wrong. Every minute of every day there are online troll-bots doing the nasty bidding of malicious clowns like David Brock, who spend millions creating a constant avalanche of fake news designed to foment hate towards my family and myself. I laugh.

Complicated, convoluted, often totally incomprehensible lies about me are concocted and then amplified, to no end, by a smug Greek chorus of corporate and leftist media hyenas holed up at the usual dreck-peddling fake news outlets like the *Washington Post*, *Salon*, *Daily Beast*, *Politico*, *Huffington Post*, *Vice*, *Slate*, and too many other leftist propaganda factories to mention here. It makes me smile.

As the Nietzschean meditation that became G. Gordon Liddy's mantra instructs us, "That which does not kill me makes me stronger."

Legendary football coach Vince Lombardi said it best, though: "Quitters never win, and winners never quit!"

Life is cyclical particularly in the political arena. You will know great victories and ignominious defeats. You will experience great thrills and great disappointments.

Today's defeat can plant the seeds of tomorrow's victory.

"It is far better to strive and fail than not to try at all," I'd say from my forty-year experience in the political arena.

When times are darkest, I remember the perseverance of Franklin Roosevelt in his fight against Polio; Winston Churchill in his wilderness years; and, of course, Richard M. Nixon's comeback from multiple political defeats.

STONE'S RULE #14

NEVER BE SCARED OF ANYONE OR ANYTHING.

Frank Sinatra said, "The big lesson in life, baby, is never be scared of anyone or anything."

Frank didn't get to be Chairman of the Board by avoiding risks and being afraid to fail. No politician or political operative ever did, either.

Like Frank, I do it my way. You should, too.

Let nothing stand in your way. Be the man or woman in the arena.

STONE'S RULES

PART #2

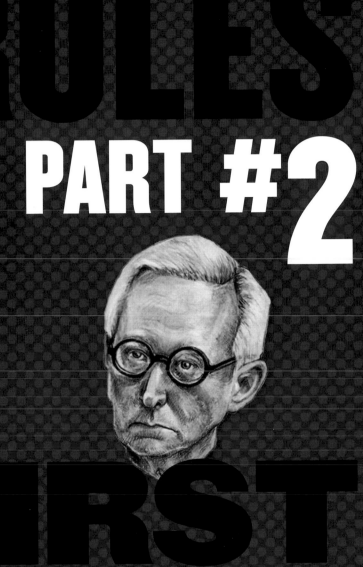

FIRST
IMPRESSIONS

IF YOU ARE ENGAGED IN ANY BUSINESS OR PROFESSION, YOU ARE MUCH MORE LIKELY TO SUCCEED IF YOU ARE WELL DRESSED THAN IF YOU ARE BADLY DRESSED.

An impression is made based on how you are dressed. It's how you present yourself, how the world sees you. No one will hire you if you are slovenly with unpolished shoes, unpressed suits with baggy knees, unkempt hair, gaudy jewelry, and less than perfect hygiene.

Dress for success!

ROGER JASON STONE, JR.
Eastern Regional Campaign Director, Reagan-Bush Committee

I learned at the knee of Dick Nixon, and helped to elect Ronald Reagan.
(Photo courtesy of Nydia Stone)

RULE #16

THE ONLY THING WORSE IN POLITICS THAN BEING WRONG IS BEING BORING.

Politics is entertainment.

Only an ivory tower policy wonk or a radical leftist militant—the insufferable Marxist type comes to mind—is simultaneously arrogant and delusional enough to think that people:

1. Have time or patience for fruitless complications and complexity in their politics (or their lives, for that matter).
2. Will suffer tedious technocrats longer than they would a commercial break on TV.
3. Give a shit about politicians' or community organizers' tedious plans for the universe or, generally, for complicated schemes being peddled by political schemers.

When you bore the voters by saying nothing new and by taking no public risks with bold ideas or proposals that shake up the status quo, the bored voters tend to look elsewhere for ideas and candidates they do find interesting.

A front runner cannot sit on a lead and serve up mush. Politics requires motion.

"The only thing worse than being wrong is being boring," Nixon told me.

When it comes to your image and your style, being bland is analogous to being boring. Just like being a bore, if you present a bland image, if you lack a personal style, it is not that people remember you as bland or boring—it is that they don't remember you at all.

LOOK GOOD.
FEEL GREAT.

Politics is like theater. An actor has confidence when he knows he is perfectly costumed, made-up and lit for the boards or film.

Knowing that your hat has just the right tilt, your collar lays perfectly, your tie is jauntily knotted, your suit emphasizes your upper body development (either through visits to the gym or excellent tailoring), you have a tan, good haircut, extremely limited jewelry, and the knowledge that you cut a fine jib, will make you feel great.

Only when you feel great can you crush those who oppose you on the battlefield. Napoleon, who had some pretty cool clothes, made his worst decisions when plagued with hemorrhoids, although riding on horseback for hundreds of miles leading an army probably added to his problem.

If you don't look great, you can't feel great. If you don't feel great, you can't make good decisions. If you don't feel great, you can't be great.

SOLID SARTORIAL ADVICE.

An old English guide to fashion I once read said, "Never spend a shilling when sixpence will suffice, never purchase anything not absolutely needful, waste nothing, and economize on clothes by taking due care of them."

RULE

#18

WHITE SHIRT + TAN FACE = CONFIDENCE.

When John F. Kennedy arrived in Chicago for the first Presidential debate in 1960, he spent the afternoon not with briefing books and closeted with aides but on the roof of his Chicago hotel with two bucksome young ladies, sunbathing. When Kennedy entered the NBC studio for the debate, journalist Theodore H. White wrote, "He looked like a bronzed god."

Nixon got to Chicago late, looking tired, haggard, and underweight from recent knee surgery and famously refused make up. He also wore a light colored, three-buttoned sack suit.

JFK looked tan and confident. Nixon looked pale and rattled.

Before an important meeting or speech, I will always get some rays and wear a white suit to accentuate the contrast and create the aura of good health and athleticism. No matter the climate, if the sun is shining you can get a little color from a half hour in the sun. A sun burn, however, will show that you're trying too hard.

STONE'S RULE #19

GREAT LEADERS HAVE PERSONAL STYLE.

There is one thing that sets a leader apart from the rest: a personal style.

FDR's naval cape with the frog closures; MacArthur's aviator frames and oversized corn cob pipe; Churchill's polka-dot bow ties and impresario Panama hat; Eisenhower's waist-length military jacket; Anthony Eden's mustache; Lincoln's stove-pipe hat; Patton's ivory handled pistols ("Only a pimp in a whorehouse would have pearl handles," said Patton).

A leader of men wants to establish differentness. Franklin Roosevelt wore *pince-nez* glasses long after they were fashionable. Herbert Hoover fished in a coat and tie and still made fly-casting look effortless. Reagan was never without his pocket handkerchief folded square and perpendicular to the line of the top of the pocket 1950s style and used pomade to hold his thick hair in place long after it was in common use, giving it a wet look. Roosevelt used a cigarette holder, as did Tom Dewey. JFK's hair was tousled just so.

Are these affectations or idiosyncrasies? I think they are just natural style.

Above all, they avoid the sameness of the masses, a world where most dress alike, eat alike, and live alike. They help create for the leader a mystique that is key to leadership.

A real leader always maintains some mystery.

BEING WELL DRESSED DOESN'T TAKE TIME.

It is a mistake to suppose that it is a waste of time to dress well. A well-dressed man need not spend any more time in dressing than a badly dressed man does.

STONE'S RULE #20

USE A CIGAR.

Vaudevillians knew that using a cigar while doing stand up gave a comedian time to think on his feet, while taking an excessively long time to light the cigar or an exaggerated puff.

While it doesn't work for elected officials, I have used a cigar for intense television interviews, such as my appearance on New York City's cable news network, New York 1, after allegations that I had made a threatening phone call to New York Governor Eliot Spitzer's 82-year old father regarding illegal campaign loans he had made financing his son's political career.

Nothing beats a large, slow-burning stogie to give you time to consider each question and formulate your response.

RULE #21

GREAT LEADERS ARE DETACHED.

Great leaders always pose themselves as detached from the political process. Charles De Gaulle, Ronald Reagan, and Franklin Roosevelt were always "big picture" guys who let minions handle the gritty details of campaigning or governing. Trump is a big picture guy in this way.

Donald Trump's campaign was a big picture vision of America's return to greatness, along similar lines to Reagan's 1980 campaign. Once the pillars of his campaign were articulated and communicated to voters, details were of very little importance.

Jimmy Carter's micromanagement of the government, down to such minutiae as scheduling use of the White House tennis courts, made him incompetent as a chief executive. Reagan probably didn't know that the White House even had tennis courts, nor did he care, yet Reagan was a highly successful chief executive. Carter bungled the Iranian hostage rescue attempt, while Reagan went on to win the Cold War.

Detachment should not be read as isolation. Nixon isolated himself behind his aides once he became president, limiting his political feel for the country and ultimately contributing to his downfall. No Congressman, senator, or even Cabinet member could get in to see President Nixon except in the most formal and predetermined of circumstances.

George H. W. Bush was so isolated from anyone who wasn't a multi-millionaire or influential Beltway so-and-so that he had never even laid eyes on the newly ubiquitous barcode scanners being used in all supermarkets and grocery stores across the country. Worse, Bush was actually dumb enough to say so. At the same time, Bush would often absent-mindedly read his stage-directions out loud, as he did in 1992 when campaigning in New Hampshire, saying, "Message: I care."

Barack Obama started down the same path when, after sweeping the middle-scheduled 2008 Democratic primaries, he responded to charges that he was long on oratory and light on specifics by saying, "Now this is a different speech with a lot more details—and a lot fewer applause lines."

Great leaders are detached, but not disconnected.

RULE #22

BUILD A FOUNDATION FOR YOUR WARDROBE.

The foundation of every young gentleman's wardrobe should be a well-cut navy suit, a solid medium gray or charcoal suit, either a navy or gray striped suit (muted, chalk, or beaded stripes), a navy blue blazer in two- or three-button models, a pair of gray flannel trousers, two generously cut pairs of khaki trousers, and a Harris tweed sports jacket in dark brown or gray.

For the slightly older gentleman, the basics can be augmented with an additional striped suit (in either blue or gray) and a double-breasted blazer, which could be navy blue or bottle green but must have military style gold buttons.

Rotate your suits, sports jackets, and blazers; be sure never to wear the same garment two days in a row. Buy high quality wooden hangers and keep your clothes in good order. Hang suits, jackets, and trousers in a well-ventilated area. Never hang a jacket or trousers on a peg or a hook.

CHEAP UNDERWEAR IS EVEN A GREATER MISTAKE WITH MEN THAN WITH WOMEN.

Your undergarments are the foundation of your wardrobe. Whether you like tighty-whities or boxer shorts, buy quality. I myself prefer a tastefully striped cotton boxer short from Charvet. Calvin Klein and 2XIST make high quality banana hammocks if you are so inclined, but I like my junk to breathe.

THE BLAZER IS THE FOUNDATION OF A GENTLEMAN'S WARDROBE.

The navy blue blazer is the most fundamental component of a gentleman's wardrobe. It can be dressed up with a neck tie and gray flannel trousers, dressed down in an open necked Brooks Brothers cotton button-down shirt and wide-cut khakis, or dressed down further with a French cut T-shirt and well-fitting jeans (indispensable for travel). The blazer should have two or three buttons of the gold military style or flat metallic buttons like Porfirio Ariza Rubirosa, the legendary playboy, race car driver, and Dominican diplomat, and always worn with a simple knit tie.

NO BOLO TIES EAST OF THE MISSISSIPPI.

Western wear is fine in the West. Unless you're trying to look like Elvis Costello or Chris Isaak, bolo ties should not be worn east of the Mississippi River.

I can appreciate the Western wear made by the rodeo tailor, Nudie, for every country star from Tex Ritter to Elvis Presley, but those are costumes.

Western shirts, belts, and cowboy hats are fine for real wranglers, but when you wear them in Washington or New York City you look like a hick.

RULE #24

THE SUIT.

The two-piece man suit, originally called a "lounge suit" or a "business suit," is still the standard for a white-collar class gentleman. Believe it or not, some suits sold today are not sewn together but rather fused, which essentially means they are glued together.

The high temperatures used in dry cleaning causes this glue to melt, which is why sometimes you see bubbling from the facing of the glued components of your jacket. Fused garments should be avoided all together and a gentleman must insist on a suit that is, at worst, machine sewn, and for a few more dollars includes some hand stitching for the lapels and collar.

The well-cut suit is your armor. This is what marks you as a master of the universe. Somber shades of blue and gray connote understated good taste.

Above all make sure your suit fits. Throughout these rules, you may find certain annotations about men's tailoring—so, good God man, make sure your clothes fit!

Different silhouettes and styles of tailoring more closely fits certain body types. The closely cut, high armhole Italian style is good for the tall lean man but not complementary for his more portly brother. The soft-shouldered, Ivy League two-button American cut works best for stocky men. The tall man should avoid vertical stripes while the fat man should avoid them in horizontal. Chose the style of tailoring that is best for your build.

AVOID DRY CLEANING.

I'm sure the American Association of Dry Cleaners would hate me, but the harsh chemicals used in dry cleaning will break down the fabrics in the finest garments over time. Fibers that are dyed navy blue, black, or dark gray are already stressed by holding the dye. Dry cleaning dries the fabric out, which is why suits cleaned in this manner begin to shine.

Unless you happen to sweat profusely, suits can be cleaned by dipping a whisk broom in cool water and gently brushing the suit. Put outside in fresh air but not direct sunlight to dry. It is essential that a suit or jacket and trousers be allowed to air out immediately after a wearing. Unless you are a slob, you should only need to clean a suit twice a year if worn in regular rotation.

RULE #25

A BLACK SQUARE-BOTTOMED KNITTED SILK TIE IS A NECESSITY.

You could roll it up in your pocket. It doesn't wrinkle. You can use it for emergency meeting in which a tie is *de riguer* and still look good. It goes with everything. In a pinch, you could use it as a belt. In an emergency, you can use it to tie a broken suitcase closed.

No resourceful gentlemen should be without one. It is truly indispensable.

RULE

#26

BUILD A FOUNDATION FOR YOUR WARDROBE.

Look at Nixon's tie knot in the 1960 debate. It has no discernable shape. Now look at Kennedy's. Tiny, elegant, and jaunty.

Whether you prefer the enormous knots favored by the Italians but pioneered by Edward VIII, the Duke of Windsor, who wanted his tie knots "thick as pudding," or you prefer the four-in-hand with perfect dimple—a tie knot must sit in the collar properly.

Congressman Jack Kemp, Reverend Adam Clayton Powell Jr., George Patton, George Raft, and Calvin Coolidge all used a neat collar pin to make the tie knot sit at the right angle. It's a look that will never go out of style if the collar pin is small and discrete and of the finest silver or gold.

RULE

#27

THE CUT OF THE SUIT MATTERS.

When LBJ became vice president, he promptly ordered, six custom made suits from Carr, Son, and Worr of Savile Row, London, who made suits for the Kennedys. In John Kennedy's case, he wore the suit, but in Johnson's case, the suit wore him.

Kennedy made his clothes wearing look effortless and casual while Johnson always looked like a gangly country boy in expensive duds.

One need not spend a fortune to have a well-cut suit. If you can't afford custom, buy the highest quality garment you can, eschewing a garment that is fused. Now, take your suit to a fine custom tailor who does alterations rather than the seamstress at the department store where you bought your suit. He can alter to your body.

Always remember it's the silhouette when seen from head to toe that matters.

REMEMBER THE SILHOUETTE.

The key thing to remember about a suit is the silhouette. Ideally, there should be an unbroken line from the skirt of the jacket to the cuff of the trouser. That's why trousers look better suspended from the shoulder rather than cinched at the waist.

STONE'S RULE #28

NEVER HOLD A MEETING UNLESS YOU KNOW WHAT RESULT YOU WANT OUT OF THE MEETING.

In both politics and business, the amount of labor and time wasted in meetings is huge.

It never ceases to shock me when I attend a meeting only to find out halfway into it that the organizers have no agenda and, by the end of it, have reached resolution on absolutely nothing.

A strong leader meticulously plans and methodically orchestrates meetings in order to achieve a desired result, or he doesn't hold them.

STONE'S RULE #29

BE ON TIME.

Nick Ruwe, Richard Nixon's long time traveling aide, advance man, and later ambassador to Iceland under Ronald Reagan, knew the 1968 Nixon campaign was meticulous about being on time for Nixon's public schedule.

On the opposite end of the candidate punctuality spectrum would be the all-time worst presidential loser Hillary Clinton, who would sometimes show up two hours late for scheduled appearances.

Ruwe, the scion of a wealthy Grosse Pointe, Michigan family, said Nixon would be on time for all public event, except rallies where he would be EXACTLY thirty minutes late to give the "warm-up man," often Johnny Grant, time to whip the crowds of Republican faithful into a frenzy.

Whenever you met Ruwe for lunch at the 21 Club you had to be EXACTLY on-time, as scheduled. Ruwe would look at his watch with satisfaction, take a drag of his cigarette and say, "Nixon men."

Whether the appointment is big or small, be like Nixon, not Clinton—always on time.

RULE #30

IMPORTANT MEETING? BLUE SUIT.

The color blue connotes authority. A well-cut, dark blue suit is required for any public performance where creditability and authority are key. When JFK showed up at the first 1960 Presidential Debate in a somber blue, muted, wide-striped suit and Vice President Richard Nixon showed up in a medium gray suit and a medium gray tie, it was already all over.

John Kennedy's navy blue two-buttoned suit was to become the new American style. Nipped at the waist and building the shoulders, it was in fact tailored in London, but the look was athletic and all-American.

We know what happened.

YOUR PANTS HAVE TO FIT.

Trousers should not fit tightly, nor should they be too loose at the seat. Baggy pants are reserved for clowns and vaudeville comedians, yet a full cut trouser which is suspended properly from the waist with braces (suspenders) should never look baggy.

Agentleman can wear a navy blue suit with brown shoes. The Italians do it and with a highly polished calfskin brogue it has flair. Dressier black lace-ups such as cap-toes or wingtips can wear as well. A navy suit is really too formal for slip-ons or loafers, which should be worn in tandem with sports jackets and the odd trouser.

A tan suit and black shoes, on the other hand, should be avoided. The tan color in an appropriate weight cloth is essentially a summer suit and black shoes would be too heavy for summer use. This is where the two-tone spectator shoe or even white bucks can be worn.

Grey Flannel, Brown Suede Shoes, Yes!

When the Duke of Windsor visited the United States by steamship in the 1930's, he arrived wearing a grey flannel suit with brown reverse-calf shoes.

Now called suede, an elegant brown suede shoe, whether it be monk strap, brogue, cap-toe, or even wing tipped, is appropriate with grey flannel trousers or a grey suit.

It is a sophisticated look preferred, along with their enormous tie knots, by the Italians.

It just works.

TWO-TONED SHOES AND WHITE BUCKS ONLY AFTER MEMORIAL DAY.

Two-toned shoes, often called spectators, are a classic look from the 1920s and '30s that still work well with a summer suit as long as the shoe is of the highest quality buck leather or suede.

Two-toned shoes draw attention to the feet and look best balanced with a Panama or high-quality straw hat.

They are ideal with searsucker cord linen or Shantung silk summer suitings in single and double-breasted styles.

Frank Nitti wore them. So did Ronald Reagan and Gary Cooper. Adolphe Menjou wore them. So did David, the Duke of Windsor.

Under no circumstances, however, should they have been worn at any time—even Halloween—except between Memorial Day and Labor Day.

STONE'S RULE #33

A BLACK SUIT SHOULD ONLY BE WORN BY CHAUFFEURS OR UNDERTAKERS.

Yes, I know that a lot of the Hollywood types like the black suit for an evening excursion of clubbing, theatre, or see-and-be-seen restaurants. I have seen them at the Ivy on Robertson. Black is too flat by itself and a black suit, white shirt, and black tie will only make you look like a chauffeur, undertaker, or Mr. Smith in *The Matrix*.

That is not to say that a black turtle-neck sweater and tight black leather pants with motorcycle boots, a Steve McQueen look, isn't great for guys under thirty-five looking to get laid.

The tuxedo, which is properly called a "dinner suit" or "evening suit," is a formal and dressy garment. What man doesn't look good in a tux?

Best choice are peaked lapels or, better yet, a shawl collar. Both styles are particularly elegant when executed in a double-breasted style by a fine designer like Alan Flusser Custom Clothing in New York.

Midnight blue is the truly correct color, as true black has a tendency to look flat and even dark green under certain lights.

Trump was an honored guest at my wedding, and I at his. (Photo courtesy of Nydia Stone.)

RULE

HANG A NAME ON YOUR OPPONENT.

#35

Conservative Florida Democratic Senator George Smathers, who was JFK's closest personal friend in Congress, took on Senator Claude Pepper in the Democratic primary for the Senate in 1950. Smathers branded Pepper as "Red Pepper," a moniker that stuck when voters learned of his liberal views on foreign affairs and civil rights.

Smathers pounded "Red Pepper" as a friend of Stalin and, if not a communist, at least a "fellow traveler."

Dick Nixon took a lesson and branded his Senate opponent, liberal actress and Congresswoman Helen Gahagan Douglas (wife of movie actor Melvyn Douglas), the "Pink Lady." "She was pink right down to her underwear," said Nixon.

I learned much about this maneuver from James L. Martin. Jim was a good ol' boy Florida political operative who engineered the election of conservative Republican Congressman Ed Gurney to the Senate in 1968 over popular former governor Leroy Collins, a moderate incumbent governor.

"Liberal Leroy," Martin branded Collins in the aggressive campaign that accentuated the few liberal stances Collins could be said to have supported.

Gurney became the first Republican elected to the US Senate from Florida since Reconstruction.

Jim Martin, an understudy of the legendary Richard Viguerie, taught me most of what I know about direct mail advertising and how to communicate a conservative message to donors and activists.

The rest I learned from my ex-wife Ann E.W. Stone. Jim and Ann are two of the most brilliant marketers I know. Martin showed in Florida that he knows how to win.

In the 2016 presidential race, Donald Trump proved to be a master of this maxim. Who will ever forget Trump's stinging and often hilarious nicknames for his opponents, particularly Jeb Bush and Ted Cruz? "Low Energy Jeb" and "Lyin' Ted" sure won't. Neither will "Crooked Hillary," whose nickname has outlasted her bitter defeat by the wily Trump, proof positive of the enduring value of this rule.

Yes, Ronald Reagan wore a brown suit. But Reagan's had a micro-thin light blue stripe, looking kind of like the upholstery in a '48 DeSoto.

Brown is flat and unflattering for most skin types—it is truly the color of shit. Solid brown suits and brown ties should generally be avoided—unless you are bold enough to match a brown knit tie with a pink button down shirt and a tiny hound's tooth brown suit.

In 1966 when Ronald Reagan ran for governor of California, I was fourteen years old. I visited and stayed with a maiden aunt in Sacramento so I could volunteer at the Reagan headquarters. Reagan was challenging Governor Edmund G. "Pat" Brown. We had bumper stickers that said, "If it's Brown—flush it!"

Now that Congressman Adam Schiff is on the scene, this can be adjusted to, "If it's Schiff—flush it!"

Sometimes you don't have to hang a name on your opponent, their name does the work for you . . . and that's no bullSchiff!

RULE #37

TO SEE HOW A CANDIDATE WILL PERFORM IN OFFICE, LOOK AT THEIR CAMPAIGN.

Winston Churchill noted that the character of a political leader could be evaluated in the rough and tumble of an election campaign.

A candidate who is sure-footed, confident, and organized will govern the same way.

A candidate who is risk-averse, poorly organized, or intellectually lazy will likewise govern the same way.

Candidates who are too rabid for power, and can't mask this flaw, will surely bring it to any public office they hold.

Candidates who have proven their abilities and skills in some other professional realm before they entered politics, and do not crave a political position or office in order to be successful, make the best leaders (Eisenhower, Reagan, and Trump come to mind).

The finest custom-tailored suit or a well-cut, low-cost Italian suit can both give a sophisticated impression to a would-be client or in a meeting with a power broker.

Nevertheless, the look can be ruined with the wrong footwear. Shoes must be one hundred percent leather or suede. No plastic, no stacked heels, no metal ornaments except for the horse bit, and these are only acceptable on genuine Gucci loafers.

Stick to capped toes, brogues, wing tips (although not at the beach, as Nixon fancied). Traditional Bass Weejun penny loafers or tasteful light Italian slip-ons of the softest leather are fine.

The Peal line of shoes made for Brooks Brothers for many years is still the standard of excellence when acquiring affordable, proper, simple, and tasteful gentlemen's footwear.

Remember: the lighter the shoe, the more elegant the look. Heavy soles, favored by the Italians, are an artsy look that may fly in the East Village or Santa Monica or Geneva, but it won't cut it for business wear even though some are very well made.

Athletic wear is never right in a business situation. Even Jay-Z puts on the custom English tailoring when he is cutting a mega-deal. Shoes must be highly polished and in excellent condition. I would never hire a man who was fastidiously dressed but was wearing scuffed shoes.

Various shades of brown suede are acceptable for those Continental Boulevardiers who want a more sophisticated look. Monkstraps or side-gusset slip-ons are strong with gray flannel and even pinstripes add a country influence to an in-town look.

George Frazier, the famous Boston columnist, said, "How to size a man up? Look down."

IF YOU SPLATTERED YOUR PATENT LEATHER EVENING PUMPS WITH MUD WHEN GOING OUT IN BLACK TIE, WIPE WITH CHAMPAGNE, NOT VASELINE.

Seriously! Champagne is the best for cleaning when bringing a luster to patent leather, and the best thing is you can drink it while you're using it to clean the shoes.

Napoleon's Partisans would work undercover while wearing a red, white, and blue-ribbon cockade that signified their allegiance to the little corporal who would become emperor.

The cockade insignia would be concealed under their lapels and inside their hats, allowing them to readily reveal themselves to other Partisans while still cloaking their activities and their loyalties to the rest of the world.

The larger lesson is well taken: sometimes it is best to cloak your real political intentions, so you are able to accomplish more without being under suspicion.

UTILIZE FINISHING TOUCHES.

The well-dressed man knows that finishing touches can impact a gentlemanly tone to one's appearance. The right pocket square, a tattersall waistcoat (vest), deeply pleated gray flannel trousers, a "paperclip" watch-chain, a tasteful pinky ring with the family crest (or a crest you invent for yourself if your family doesn't have one).

Now that your foot is in the door and you've made an impression, it's time to capitalize and strike.

STONE'S RULES

PART #3

GOING ON THE ATTACK

ATTACK

RULE #41

ATTACK, ATTACK, ATTACK – NEVER DEFEND.

This was the credo of the late Murray Chotiner, one tough Jew who was the real Jedi Master of negative attack politics.

Chotiner made Earl Warren governor of California and put Bill Knowland in the Senate. But most importantly, he was *eminence-griese* for Congressman, Senator, Vice-President, and President Richard Milhous Nixon.

Operating in the days before television, Chotiner refined and perfected the modern negative campaign, relentlessly attacking his opponents in flyers, radio commercials, voter mailings, and telephone calls.

Murray and his brother were both lawyers, representing dozens if not hundreds of mid-level hoods and gunsels throughout the 1950s and '60s. Nixon White House Chief of Staff H. R. 'Bob' Haldeman observed that Chotiner had "the nerves of a cat burglar."

When dealing with a sticky public situation with charges flying, Murray was adamant about the only course of action:

1. If it is necessary to issue a denial of charges leveled against you, do it quickly and only do it once!
2. Avoid repeating the charges, anywhere, ever.
3. Counter attack with greater ferocity!

RULE

LET NO ATTACK GO UNANSWERED.

#42

Bill Clinton recognized that every attack must be answered.

But this is not the same as launching a defense, which would violate Murray Chotiner's rule of "attack and never defend."

Any attack must be answered only as an element of a devastating counterattack.

Be careful not to repeat the charge in full or in any detail. It is never wise to educate that portion of the voters who have not yet heard the scurrilous charges against you.

In this age of the internet and twenty-four-hour cable news networks—of instant information—news travels quickly, so "rapid response" is a twenty-four-hour-a-day task and a critical element to have securely in place, ready to go at a moment's notice. A campaign without such a mechanism is doomed.

I learned this from the legendary Frank Hague, the boss of Jersey City and Hudson County, New Jersey. Frank "I am the law" Hague ran the city and county with an iron fist, assiduously addressing the political concerns of the Irish, Italians, Poles, Hungarians, African Americans, and a smattering of Puerto Ricans whose votes Hague controlled.

Hague was a legendary planner who worked each of these ethnic constituencies with patronage and, for those who were recalcitrant, muscle.

Have a plan.

Work your plan—every day, every hour, every minute you are not sleeping. And when you are asleep, dream about your plan and how you can better work it.

Don't be afraid to change it when circumstances change.

In the Nixon White House, any aide summoned to the office of Chief of Staff H. R. 'Bob' Haldeman who didn't bring a pad with him was summarily fired.

Whether it is on an old-school yellow legal pad or a personal electronic device of any sort, make a list of your tasks.

If you prefer to go the traditional route with a pad, be sure to carry a fine leather jotter in your inside breast pocket.

Revise and review your task list every day. Be relentless in your follow up.

Cross off action items from your list as you complete them.

ZERO DEFECTS as Haldeman demanded—let nothing fall through the cracks.

RULE #45

PLANS ARE WORTHLESS, PLANNING IS INDISPENSABLE.

Eisenhower said it.

Candidates or clients who demand ornate written plans for an advertising and public relations or electoral military campaign don't understand that life is not a static process and that any written plan would have to be amended as circumstances swiftly change—making the written plan time consuming and ultimately useless.

Leadership is adaptive according to changing circumstances, and thus decision making must be somewhat ad hoc. Franklin Roosevelt, whose biography by Lord Conrad Black (a rogue of the first order) I like, had no plan when he vowed to bring America back from depression.

FDR improvised a series of ad hoc decisions and initiatives that brought back America's confidence and ultimately her strength. Roosevelt had setbacks, like the defeat of his effort to expand the Supreme Court.

Knowing what direction you want to head is about tactics. Knowing what you want to achieve is a clearly defined goal. Having a strategy to get there is crucial. Inviolable plans are worthless.

Planning, on the other hand, knowing ahead of time how you will cross a river and low long it will take if the time to cross the river should come, is a different thing entirely. Logistical planning is crucial.

RULE #46

ATTACK YOUR ENEMY ON MANY FRONTS.

To vanquish an enemy at war or to win a political campaign, you must attack your opponent on many fronts.

Your opponent must be *and* feel not only besieged, but also confused and demoralized.

Superior planning and lightning speed in the thrust of your attacks will dominate the race, put your opponent off balance, and cause them to make errors, only compounding your opportunities to attack them again and again.

Open many fronts, force your opponent to fight every battle, and you will win the war.

THE BIG LIE TECHNIQUE.

Erroneously attributed to Nazi propaganda chief Joseph Goebbels, the "big lie" manipulation technique was actually first described in detail by Adolf Hitler himself. Though it would be convenient to characterize it as Nazi self-revelation, the truth is that Hitler was using it to describe what he called "Jewish calumny," among other things.

Nonetheless, the tactic of creating a lie so bold, massive, and even so monstrous that it takes on a life of its own, is alive and well all through American politics and news media. Make it big, keep it simple, repeat it enough times, and people will believe it.

This big lie technique is precisely how the Democrat Party and its mainstream media handmaidens reacted to the 2016 election and the improbable defeat dealt them by Donald J. Trump.

The media's mindless, yet endless, insistence that the Russian state helped Donald Trump win, along with the completely bogus claims that Julian Assange is a Russian agent and that I received supposedly hacked emails from Wikileaks and then passed them to Donald Trump and the Trump campaign, is truly the biggest Big LIE of the century.

The reality is that the Democrat-contrived Russia-Trump collusion hoax has at its core nothing more than a wishful left-wing conspiracy theory inflated, exploited, expanded, and repeated over and over and over, for nearly two years. Yet, still, these partisan media hacks and their fellow Democrat deception artists in Congress produced absolutely ZERO evidence to substantiate any of their defamatory insinuations, or to justify the false, misleading distraction all this has been to American political life.

But, then, was this not really the whole point of it? To distract, divert, defame, delay, and ultimately destroy President Trump and the progress he has been making on so many fronts? The deranged talking-head pygmies at MSNBC, the effete snobs at *Salon*, *Daily Beast*, *Vice*, and other leftist propaganda fronts shamelessly peddled this garbage without the slightest intention of ever producing any actual evidence to back up any of their cacophonous din of aspersions, disguised as speculative reporting.

Of course, this mass journalistic malpractice is supplemented by a veritable army of online troll-bots directed by America's sleaziest troll-bot of all, the repugnant Clinton mercenary David Brock, head of the subversive Media Matters. Brock runs what is an industrial-grade disinformation operation that exists solely to reinforce their BIG LIE.

I believe in a belt *and* suspenders, at least when it comes to getting your campaign message out.

When communicating a message in today's media diversity, you must wage your campaign in *every* medium, looking for the pick up that will catapult your message to a greater audience to achieve your public relations and political messaging goals.

People often ask me which medium is most important today—social media, television, mailers, etc.

My answer is simply: ALL of them.

When getting your message out to the world, leave no stone unturned. (Pun intended)

THE KEY WORD IN CHOOSING YOUR WARDROBE IS "APPROPRIATE."

Knowing when and where to attack your enemy is just as important as dressing for the activity you will be engaged in. For instance, don't wear madras shorts at a wedding and don't show up in a tuxedo for bowling. Never wear athletic wear any place other than a gym or while engaged in some organized outdoor sport. Never go shopping dressed in athletic wear—sales people will assume you are penniless and the service will suck.

Don't be afraid of iconic items such as buttery soft Gucci loafers and a Hermes belt.

RULE
#50

MIX PATTERNS BUT NOT PURPOSE.

Clothing is either formal, casual, or sports oriented. These elements of dress cannot be mixed. A dark navy blue, double-breasted suit requires a starched cutaway or long point collar, a small patterned tie, colors to the taste of the wearer, but buttoned-down collars or sport shirts won't mix—the only exception being the black cashmere turtle-neck—which, let's face it, is so cool it can be worn with anything.

Buttoned-down shirts, khaki slacks, ribbon belts, and Bass Weejun penny loafers are casual attire that can be dressed up or down with a neck tie, but never appropriate for business.

STONE'S RULE #51

CASUAL DRESS DOES NOT EXCUSE YOU FROM GOOD TASTE.

First of all, all-natural fibers: cotton, linen, wool are acceptable. Khakis, chinos, polo shirts, solid colored T-shirts. Synthetic blends of any kind are unacceptable, except in socks where it's needed for resiliency.

Shorts should be khaki, black, navy blue, seersucker, or madras and should fall just above the knee. Hotpants are never acceptable for men who are not in drag. Shorts are never worn with a sports coat or blazer unless vesting Bermuda.

Esquire correctly points out that the closest a man should come to denim shorts is helping a lady out of them.

Dress khakis up with a blazer and down with a T-shirt.

Sports jerseys are for professional athletes; if you aren't one, don't wear one. Rugby shirts are for guys under forty.

Ribbon style belts and watch bands can prep up a look and give you a break from highly polished leather belts and braces (known in the US as "suspend-ers" and should never be clip-on.)

Hats with any team or tractor company logo will mark you as a "Country fuck," as Eddie Murphy said in *24 Hours*.

RULE

DON'T GET MAD.
GET EVEN.

#52

If you have never been screwed over, one way or another, you have never operated in real-world politics. For many political creatures, screwing over others is an art form, if not a second career.

Franklyn 'Lyn' Nofziger, Ronald Reagan's long-time press secretary and fiercely loyal political aide, would get even with anyone he felt was hurting the Gipper. Reagan biographer Lou Cannon wrote that the disheveled Nofziger looked like a "wax pear that sat on the radiator too long."

During a briefing for Reagan delegates in 1976, one of us asked what "our demeanor should be on the floor." Nofziger replied: "The de meaner, de better."

Always be ready to display ferocity, but never true anger. The reality is that anger distracts and can cause even the coolest of politicians to make mistakes—sometimes big ones. Richard Nixon would rage against his opponents and issue orders (some even illegal) to

Chief of Staff Bob Haldeman. An experienced Nixon hand, Haldeman knew not to act on any of it, as Nixon would reverse himself once he cooled off.

As a genuine emotion, anger is wasteful and enervating. But as a purposeful, planned tactic, a well-placed show of anger can work wonders. Done right, it is a surefire way to instill fear in the weak and garner respect from anyone foolish enough to have underestimated the consequences of crossing you.

Pulling the "Full Sicilian"—a sudden explosion of unbridled, towering rage—should be as coldly calculated as it is terrifying, even destabilizing, to whoever is unlucky enough to be on the receiving end of it. I used to practice in front a mirror how to make the veins on my forehead pop out, as a finishing touch to my "out-of-control Italian" routine.

A true pro knows that getting even with an opponent who stuck it to you almost never happens when the sting of being screwed over is most profound. The cool-headed, well-seasoned political operator knows how to take even the worst screw job in stride and immediately begin channeling and focusing the energy of a burning anger into the task of devising an exquisitely devastating payback that will make the screwing you received look like a Sunday picnic by comparison.

The satisfaction you'll feel when you settle a righteous vendetta against some deserving, but unsuspecting, shmuck who thought they walked away scot-free after plunging a knife in your back, is an exhilaration worth every bit of the steely discipline you have to summon to quickly and calmly move past the inevitable slings and arrows of outrageous political fortune.

RULE

#53

GO FOR THE BANK SHOT.

When Senator Robert F. Kennedy was assassinated in June 1968, liberal New York Governor Nelson Rockefeller appointed moderate Republican Congressman Charles Goodell to the Senate seat left vacant by Kennedy's death. (Senator Goodell's son, Roger, is currently Commissioner of the NFL.)

For the next two years Goodell moved hard left, becoming one of the Vietnam War's most vocal critics. This drove President Nixon nuts, perhaps more so than the same criticisms coming from any anti-war Democrat.

When the seat came up for election in 1970, Goodell sought to win it in his own right. He faced two opponents. One was New York Conservative Party nominee James L. Buckley, brother of conservative icon and *National Review* founder William F. Buckley Jr. The other was multi-millionaire Democrat Congressman Richard L. Ottinger, who, like Goodell, was also a prominent critic of the war in Vietnam.

As the campaign closed in on election day, it appeared Democrat Ottinger would defeat both Buckley and Goodell. That is, until Nixon dispatched Vice President Spiro Agnew to New York to savagely attack the embarrassingly liberal Republican Goodell.

Thanks to the Republican Vice-President's sustained rhetorical bludgeoning of his own party's US Senate candidate, the anti-war vote ended up being redistributed between Ottinger and Goodell. Enough liberal anti-war voters migrated from Ottinger to Goodell that Buckley was able to squeeze past both men and win one of New York's US Senate seats, denying it to *both* major political parties.

Sometimes you *gotta* use the bank shot.

HATE IS A STRONGER MOTIVATOR THAN LOVE.

Only a candy-ass would think otherwise. People feel satisfied when there is something they can vote FOR. They feel exhilarated when there is something—or someone—they can vote AGAINST. Just ask President Hillary Clinton about all of the people who rushed out to vote FOR her.

The unfortunate, but hard, reality is that few people actually vote their hopes and aspirations. Modern American politics have seen few figures who attracted voters with an upbeat and optimistic message, convincing Americans that there was no limit to what America could do, while weathering the typical barrage of attacks from their opponents.

John Kennedy was one, with the youthful vigor of his New Frontier. Ronald Reagan clearly revived a moribund, Jimmy Carter-malaise-weary country with his soaring confidence in America as "that shining city on a hill."

There is no question that Donald Trump's central campaign theme was the most positive and upbeat since Reagan: to Make America Great Again. Trump stands with only Kennedy and Reagan in this stead.

Sorry to those who think Barack Obama was elected because his campaign was somehow distinctly positive or even that his message was the key to his success. You are being as phony as your dear leader, if you hew to this myth.

The Obama campaign was certainly awash in slick reproductions of pre-World War II national socialist propaganda art themes, loaded with highly-generic, to the point of being utterly meaningless, buzzwords.

But Obama did not rise on his message, and he most certainly did not have to weather any of the typical types of sustained assaults from his opponent(s) that every other previous presidential candidate faced and that made their ultimate victory a genuine feat, as was the case with the Kennedy, Reagan, and Trump.

While Trump's core message was uniquely inspirational, with the country coming off of the saccharin-empty high of a technocratic pseudo-messiah, Trump was also the beneficiary, and an extraordinarily deft amplifier, of a deep, and frankly much-deserved, loathing for Trump's dour and shrill opponent in 2016.

Trump perfectly epitomized how being an upbeat, inspiring cheerleader as a candidate in no way means not also being a hard-hitting brawler, when necessary, especially when the chips are down.

A winning candidate knows how to be a harsh critic without being perceived as a nasty curmudgeon. John McCain knows how to land a great zinger and has an acerbic wit. The problem is that McCain became known as more cranky curmudgeon than magnanimous, albeit caustically witty, candidate.

Do-gooders and disingenuous leftists who decry the politics of fear and negativism are simply denying the reality of human nature, and only fooling themselves. Emotions cannot simply be erased or ignored, and to believe they can is a suicidally-naive approach to political competition.

Voters may superficially tell pollsters and pundits how "turned off" they are by all of the "negative campaigning," but the reality is that voters are entertained and often-riveted by attack politics. Donald Trump transformed it into nearly an art form in 2016, and it was a key ingredient, if not the THE key ingredient of his stunning victory.

The same people who tell you they hate negative political TV commercials will also be able to tell you exactly what was in them. A political strategist's job is to exploit negative but memorable ads for the purpose of winning votes. The trick is in being able to engage in negative campaigning without being successfully cast, or widely perceived, as running a "negative campaign."

Understanding the voters' fears, apprehensions and, yes, hatred, is just as critical a part of political messaging as knowing how to appeal to their hopes and aspirations. A campaign that figures out how to do both simultaneously is the most likely to succeed.

It was W. C. Fields who said, "Hell, I always vote against—never for!"

I also advised Nixon in the 1980s. (Wikimedia Commons)

ALWAYS PRAISE 'EM BEFORE YOU HIT 'EM.

This technique was one of Dick Nixon's best. The veteran political pugilist would praise his opponent's sincerity and commend the opponent's genuine belief in what are, nonetheless, terrible ideas and repugnant ideologies.

"Praise 'em before you hit 'em— makes the hit seem more reasonable and even-handed, and thus more effective," said the Trickster.

"My friend Hubert Horatio Humphrey is a sincere liberal. I have the utmost respect for the depth of Senator Humphrey's belief in creating a more socialized America," Nixon would say.

RULE

HE WHO SPEAKS FIRST LOSES.

#56

I had a cousin on my mother's side who was in the vegetable business. He grew tomatoes, peppers, and cucumbers in South Jersey. Every morning at 5 a.m. he would drive his produce to an open-air market in Philadelphia where he would sell his vegetables at that day's going rate.

"You never tell 'em what you want for your cucumbers until they tell you what they are paying for cucumbers or you'll leave money on the table," my cousin told me.

I don't sell my cucumber until I know what a client wants to pay for it.

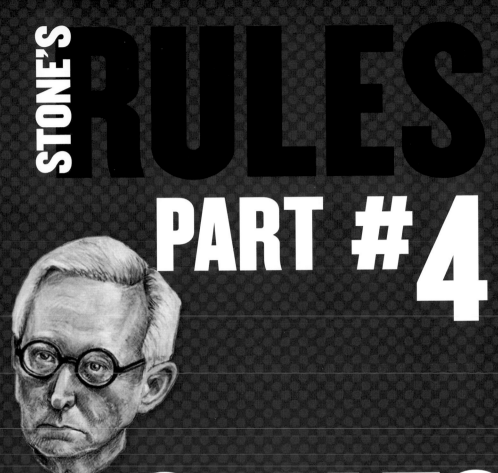

STONE'S RULES

PART #4

HOW TO WIN IN POLITICS

RULE #57

LOSERS DON'T LEGISLATE.

Politics is about winning, not going down with your flags flying.

Voters should not be viewed monolithically but broken down into various groups who respond to various appeals. Politics is about meticulously expanding your group, not about ideological purity or taking your last stand on the last hill.

If your base is happy 100 percent of the time it only proves that you are not reaching out for new voters and are stagnating on your own turf.

Learn how to stretch the limits of your base, but never betray it.

Whenever a young man or woman comes to work for me, I require them to read David Ogilvy's *Confessions of an Advertising Man*, the second greatest book ever written (after the Holy Bible).

A Scottish advertising genius, Ogilvy's principles were used in newspaper, magazine and TV advertising in the '70s and '80s with incredible success. They also apply, with equally extraordinary effect, to Internet-age messaging.

"Write great headlines and you'll have successfully invested 80 percent of your money" was one of Ogilvy's famous maxims.

Ogilvy came from the world of direct response advertising, which used devices like coupons and reply-by-mail campaigns to invoke consumer response. This way, success could be measured on more than just sales figures.

Readers can grasp bold ideas and concepts through headlines and Ogilvy favored the big, bold, stark headline. He believed the key to good advertising was in your "offer" to voters, which must be immediately discernible in your headline. Telling voters what is in it for them is the best way to grab their attention.

Signs and billboards are hit-and-run. You can only effectively communicate the name of the candidate or cause. If I see a logo without the candidate's name as the largest, most prominent feature, I see a lost opportunity.

With Internet advertising, your pitch must be long enough to tell a story, but short enough not to lose the reader's attention.

David Ogilvy was a "madman" before *Mad Men* showed the world what a "madman" was. His book revolutionized my ideas about advertising. Read it, learn it, live it.

STONE'S RULE #59

THE MORE YOU TELL, THE MORE YOU SELL.

The idea that short advertisements and heavily abbreviated advertising copy are most effective is wrong.

I learned this from James L. Martin, the direct mail advertising genius. Martin learned it from Richard Viguerie, the direct mail pioneer who, more than anyone else, figured out how to use direct marketing to rally conservatives and raise millions of dollars, in small dollar contributions for conservative causes.

The most successful fundraising letter of all time ran to twenty-six pages and was signed by George McGovern.

Thirty-second TV commercials don't give you much time to sell. Sixty-second commercials are better, but difficult to buy in prime time.

Longer direct mail, newspaper, magazine and other direct-response print advertising invariably outperform shorter copy. Unlike other forms of advertising, the effectiveness of direct-response advertising can be measured by the number of orders or contributions garnered by a specific mailing or ad piece.

Many of the very best TV and radio writers first cut their teeth in direct-response advertising. Attention spans may be short today, but when a reader does opt to engage with focus, having longer, more detailed copy ultimately gives more bang for the buck. Better to have 10 percent read the longer copy, with some real impact, than 100 percent wiz past a short copy ad, none of it sinking in, much less having an impact.

STONE'S RULE #60

SOMETIMES YOU'VE GOT TO TURN CHICKEN SHIT INTO CHICKEN SALAD.

In politics and in life, you play the cards you are dealt. Sometimes you have to take your greatest disadvantage and turn it into a plus. Lyndon Johnson called it "changing chicken shit into chicken salad."

When Nixon, who Johnson never had any particular use for and had called a "chicken shit" was elected president, LBJ released a statement of obligatory praise for Nixon, as was the custom of that era.

When reminded by reporters that he had called Nixon a 'chicken shit,' Johnson said, "He changed chicken shit into chicken salad."

Candidates should never be filmed or photographed with sun glasses. Dark sunglasses make you look sinister, not sexy, like Marcello Mastriani. Think Giacana, Onassis, and Carmine DeSapio, the legendary boss of the Manhattan Democratic Machine.

I wear them, but then, I'm not running.

PONYTAILS ARE FOR MEN UNDER 30.

A bald pate and a ponytail should require the death penalty. This odd look is seen in only three places in America: Los Angeles, New York City, and Atlantic City, NJ.

I'd embrace my baldness before I wore a Hollywood-agent ponytail while going bald.

In 2000, I went to Miami-Dade County in Florida to work on the presidential recount then underway. I went not because I was a Bush Republican, but because former Secretary of State James A. Baker III asked me to go.

In 1981, Baker overruled the White House political shop and secured President Reagan's appearance in a campaign TV commercial for New Jersey gubernatorial candidate Thomas H. Kean. Baker did this at my request (and badgering). Kean went on to win . . . by only 1200 out of 2.5 million votes. I never forgot it.

When Baker called me in 2000, the Florida recount had already been fully conducted twice, with no change in results—George W. Bush had won more votes in Florida than Vice President Al Gore, period. This is now undisputed.

Gore's partisans on the ground, directed by Beltway Democrat lawyers, were beginning to methodically and systematically drag out the recount, working to create doubts and cause delay, while they litigated and manipulated the process.

Pro-Gore actors would have done anything and everything possible to prolong the process and delay any final recount certification, for the next three-and-a-half years if necessary, as long as Gore kept coming up short.

Baker told me to shut it down.

I thought about the help Baker gave me, almost twenty years earlier, before I picked up the walkie-talkie and ordered Republican activists to storm the Miami-Dade County Courthouse—fomenting what became famously known as the "Brooks Brothers Riot."

The so-called "Brooks Brothers Riot" prevented Democrats from removing ballots to an area with no observers and halted the recounting of the same ballots for the third time.

Given the sneaky Democrat maneuvers, it was justifiable citizen action if you ask me.

Paying one's political debts is not only the right thing, it is good business. It may, and typically does, entail doing something you may not like and may not want to do. If it was something easy, it probably wouldn't be a political favor. But politics is assuredly a business in which "what goes around, comes around."

CAMPAIGN FINANCE REFORM HAS DONE FOR POLITICS WHAT PANTYHOSE HAS DONE FOR FINGER FUCKING.

Money always seeks its own level. What all of our august lawmakers in Congress know is that influence and power always have ready, eager purchasers, whose money will always find a route to its intended power broker, no matter how circuitous.

The 1974 post-Watergate campaign finance reforms (some of which were successfully challenged, for violating the First Amendment, in the US Supreme Court by Senator James L. Buckley of New York, brother of William F. Buckley and now a distinguished member of the bench), were merely circumvented through party committees and other dodges.

The more recent McCain-Feingold campaign finance law, even more ridiculously inhibitive of free speech was, thank God, functionally-circumvented by so-called '527' committees that can express political opinions, as long as they are not directly advocating the election or defeat of any candidate. Yes, even

Swift Boat Veterans for Truth and Danney Williams, Bill Clinton's abandoned son, have free speech rights.

The Citizens United decision leveled the playing field allowing corporations the same rights as unions.

Whatever the next iteration of rules the Beltway masterminds impose, as with all previous attempts it, too, will somehow be legally circumvented, because politics thrives on money.

RULE #65

USE THE INTERNET TO DO WITH THOUSANDS OF DOLLARS WHAT ONCE REQUIRED MILLIONS.

The Internet changed everything in politics by putting public office within reach of modestly financed candidates.

Yesterday's era of network TV as the only outlet for mass communications had advertising costs in the millions for a congressional race in markets like Los Angeles, New York, Miami, or Dallas, and in the tens of millions for statewide offices.

Location and interest profiling of select geotargeted voters now allows a candidate to communicate far more effectively and cost-efficiently with their target audience.

Even a $250,000 ad buy is just a drop in the bucket on network TV. But a $250,000 digital media campaign that employs sound advertising principles and uses finite geopolitical targeting can be a winner, with exponentially more bang for the buck.

Raising vast sums of money or being a millionaire capable of self-funding a campaign to purchase a seat in Congress, like New Jersey's Frank Lautenberg or Wisconsin's Herb Kohl, are no longer prerequisites to winning public office.

Now public offices are within the grasp of those not in the permanent political class or among a small few ultra-wealthy elites. The ability to reach voters electronically, at far less cost than traditional methods, is the most positive development for our Republic in at least a century.

It has also expanded the impact of millions of special interest dollars which, for better or worse, can level the playing field in David and Goliath political races, especially against incumbent politicians with lobbyist-loaded political war chests.

The democratizing effect of the Internet and unprecedented electoral successes by outsiders against a well-heeled elite ruling class have been profound, particularly for those battling left-wing dominance of mass media.

Unfortunately, to counteract this trend, hard-left executives at various tech giants have underhandedly resorted to a most heinous and un-American abuse of their monopolistic control over online information: censorship.

Years ago, when everyone was signing onto these new platforms, these companies never disclosed designs to use their unprecedented control over nearly all published information in today's online world as a tool to serve their own narrow political and ideological ends.

Once Google-YouTube, Twitter, Facebook, and other Silicon Valley Internet companies made themselves the dominant, if not nearly exclusive, channels of online information, their true colors as authoritarian ideologues quickly and garishly began to fly.

Now anyone who opposes their political dogma, exposes corruption of power (including their own), or works against their favored politicians, government schemes, or pet left-wing causes risks being digitally suppressed, if not eliminated entirely, from the virtual public square.

"Tech" has now been unmasked as the TechLeft. Their former role as mere silent, unseen facilitators of information platforms in exchange for advertising dollars has been sneakily transformed into that of censors, content-minders, political correctness enforcers, and the ultimate arbiters of online speech.

Let me be among the first to predict that this will be their ultimate undoing and that the democratizing essence of the Internet will ultimately take them down, just as it has smashed the death grip that ruling institutional elites had, for many decades, over access to public office and the political process.

RULE #66

NEVER TURN DOWN A MAJOR PARTY NOMINATION.

When Christine Todd Whitman, daughter of longtime Nixon friend, backer, and Eisenhower intimate Webster Todd Sr., told former president Richard Nixon that she could get the Republican nomination for US Senate from New Jersey against former NBA and then-current political superstar Bill Bradley, the old man told her to go for it.

"You never know what will happen and the political atmosphere can change in a second," said the "Sage of Saddle River," as Nixon came to be known in dispensing his wisdom from his modest residence in the New Jersey town of that name.

Bradley got caught in a Democratic downwash in the fall out of Governor Jim Florio's disastrous tripling of the state's income tax and just barely topped Whitman in a true squeaker of an election.

Whitman had lost, but instantaneously became the odds-on favorite for Governor in the the following year's race. Whitman took her shot, defeated a former attorney general in the GOP primary and then, in a major upset, beat the tax-hiking Democrat Florio.

No political aspirant can harm their long-term political prospects by becoming a major party nominee for any statewide or national office. Barring any serious gaffes, a truly horrible campaign, or a permanently damaging scandal, even if the candidate loses, they will become a party favorite for the next major office to open up.

They will also have gained the invaluable experience of a running a full-fledged campaign all the way to the finish line and, unless their loss was an embarrassing blowout, will have a significant fundraising advantage right from the outset of their next bid. On the upside, they may actually win the race.

Turning down such an opportunity risks the candidate's appearing to be any number of undesirable things, depending on the circumstances, from vain to craven to disloyal to self-serving to unsure to unreliable. Even if the candidate had every good reason to sit out the race, if the party is left in a lurch as a result or has to scramble to find a credible nominee, the party faithful will not soon forget, especially when the candidate comes back around, looking for the nomination of their choice.

A major party nomination for high office is a prize not to be tossed aside lightly. Do so at your own peril.

WHAT'S IN THE PUBLIC DOMAIN IS FAIR GAME.

One weekend in October 1965, almost a year after the defeat of my hero Barry Goldwater, I was taking the commuter train from New Canaan, Connecticut to New York City to volunteer in *National Review* founder William F. Buckley's campaign for Mayor.

I was present when Buckley asked what he would do if he won, said, "Demand a recount." This was a time when conservatism had fallen into political disrepute, after a year of nonstop maligning by the forces arrayed around LBJ and his reelection, some of which were involved in taking out President Kennedy to clear Johnson's path to power.

We were accused of being anti-Semites, Klansmen, red baiters, warmongers, crypto-fascists, and worse. Bill Buckley changed all that. He proved that conservatism could be charming, erudite, intellectual, and cool.

Decades later, George Pataki beat Mario Cuomo for Governor of New York, running as a tax-cutting conservative. By the end of his second term, Pataki had morphed into an out-of-control spender who had mortgaged the state's future, borrowing through so-called independent authorities to avoid getting all of this borrowing approved by New York voters, as the state's Constitution required.

Pataki ended up tripling the state's debt. He also passed the strictest gun control legislation in the country, after falsely reassuring gun owners, sportsmen, hunters and enthusiasts (of which upstate New York has many) that he supported the Second Amendment. He even declined to oppose partial birth abortion, taking a position that is closer to far left than anything resembling conservative thought.

In New York State a candidate can be nominated by more than one party, appearing as the nominee of multiple parties, beyond just Republicans and Democrats. The candidate's cumulative vote total is what matters to victory, but for purposes of distinguishing how much support each party garnered in actual votes, it is possible to break down the vote totals by party nominee.

This can prove quite useful, especially in giving leverage to smaller, more ideologically oriented parties that may well have the votes needed to give a major party candidate the necessary margin for victory.

I knew Pataki had a lock on the Conservative Party nomination for Governor.

The party has drifted far from the days when it supplied a counter balance to the liberal Republican Party of Nelson Rockefeller and Jack Javits.

With the gubernatorial race and Pataki in mind, I called Bill Buckley and he invited me to come by his Maisonette for a chat. I shared my thoughts on what a disappointment his fellow Yalie, Pataki, had been. Buckley wholeheartedly agreed. I suggested to Bill that penning his views on the governor in either the National Review or in his own nationally syndicated column would be quite useful.

Erudite and brilliant but nothing of an ivory tower intellectual, Buckley took hometown and home state politics seriously. He ended up writing several scathing pieces on Pataki. When I included Buckley's accurate quotes in mailings to Conservative Party members and leaders, I got an email from Bill that the Conservative Party hierarchy was complaining.

Having utmost respect for this founding member of the contemporary conservative political movement in America and a good friend over many years, I nonetheless replied that Bill's comments had been published, putting them squarely in the public domain and, thus, making them fair game for use elsewhere, including communications to the public in a political race.

"Right you are," responded Bill. "Come by for a drink when you are next in New York."

A TAN MAKES A MAN LOOK VIGOROUS AND A DEEP TAN MAKES A MAN LOOK PROSPEROUS.

Aristotle Onassis spent a very large amount of his time cavorting in the sun on his yacht wearing oversized sunglasses, a gold medal, slicked back hair, and a high waisted Italian bathing suit, usually accompanied by beautiful woman like Maria Callas and Jacqueline Kennedy, later Onassis. Ari said you can never be too tan.

Reagan maintained his tan through his time as a Hollywood star, television host and Governor of California. After a bout with skin cancer, Reagan's sun worship was over. Ever conscious of his appearance, Reagan would drink a small glass of red wine just before a television appearance because he knew it gave him rosy cheeks, which accentuated his Irish all-American appeal.

Having looked pale in his first debate with the bronzed JFK, by 1968 Nixon was using a sun lamp at home to have a rosy glow before major TV appearances. Nixon called it home cooking but was careful to avoid sunburns, using just enough of the lamp's rays to have a healthy glow.

There was a tanning product for men at the time called Man-tan, which, sadly, made you look orange. Today, Clinique, among other high-end brands, makes bronzers for men that will make you look rested, confident, and on top of the world, even if you over-imbibed on vodka martinis at Elaine's the night before. I highly recommend owning some.

RULE

#69

EVERYTHING IS RECYCLED.

Milton Berle once said that there are no such things as new jokes, only old jokes rewritten for the time. Uncle Miltie stole more than his share of them.

So it is with political ideas. Even innovative ideas borrow from the past. Politics in the United States are not known for public policy boldness.

All the ideas today's politicians present to the voters are simply recycled versions of the same basic formulae that have been employed by political hucksters and power-accumulating government careerists for nearly a century.

The public interest is not served, but rather diminished, by such staleness and stasis. Even the funniest jokes ever told are only so funny, by half, with each subsequent retelling.

When you have already heard the same joke or some predictable variation of it fifty times before, it is no longer just not funny, it is tiresome and tedious.

The same applies to the tired tripe that America's imperial political class has been perpetually regurgitating on the American people for the last fifty years.

Nothing is new, just refurbished for resale. But America sure could use a new set of jokes . . .

RULE #70

MOVE TO THE RIGHT FOR THE PRIMARY, MOVE TO THE CENTER FOR THE GENERAL.

Obviously the first part of the rule is stated for Republicans. If you are a Democrat, you move left for the primary. Whatever party you hail from, for the general election you move to, or at least towards, the center.

This was Nixon's formulation: secure a base first, then win the votes of Independents and Democrats. The candidate who spends the entire campaign pandering to his base will win his base, but nothing else.

Focusing on your base in the party primary is fine, but limit it to targeted communications, like direct mail. You want to motivate your base but not offend Independent and Democrat voters to whom you can appeal on other issues.

If your base is 100 percent happy with your campaign, you are probably not getting any Independent or Democratic votes.

Donald Trump achieved in Michigan, Wisconsin, Ohio, and Pennsylvania what John McCain and Mitt Romney could not.

Trump made deep in roads into blue collar, working-class Democrat voters.

Politics is about coalition building:
holding your base while, at the same
time, reaching out beyond it to win over
every vote needed for ultimate electoral
victory.

RULE #71

POLITICS IS THE ART OF ADDITION, NOT SUBTRACTION.

John Davis Lodge, my mentor, was a Congressman, governor of Connecticut, ambassador to Spain and Argentina, and both a Broadway and movie actor. Lodge taught me that politics is about adding to your coalition and not alienating any voters unnecessarily.

Often referred to as Henry Cabot Lodge's "smarter brother," Lodge was broad-chested and handsome. He was also one of the greatest swordsmen of his day, bedding Marlene Dietrich, Greta Garbo, and Myrna Loy.

Charming and gregarious, Lodge married an Italian beauty who was working as a dancer. A Catholic, Francesca Braggiotti Lodge was disdained by Lodge's Brahmin family but was a huge asset with Italian voters, who were mostly Democrats in Connecticut. Francesca danced and sang in Italian at Lodge's campaign rallies to thunderous applause.

Lodge defeated Colonel Henri Mucci, an Italian American war hero, in a heavily Italian Congressional district.

Lodge understood that politics is the art of addition.

RULE #72

FOLKS WANT TO GET GOVERNMENT OUT OF THE BOARDROOM AND THE BEDROOM.

Elections are not won on the extremes. It is why Barry Goldwater and George McGovern both went down in flames. Elections are won by securing a base and then attracting independents and persuadable voters in the center.

Ronald Reagan had a firm conservative base, but he won election with the votes of suburban moderates who correctly judged he was the right man at the right time.

President Trump's campaign similarly brought voters of many stripes together who were tired of Americans being put last by the Washington establishment.

I believe that the America's governing majority will continue to be those who are fiscally conservative, anti-tax, and pro-business while at the same time socially moderate, with pro-choice, pro-privacy, and even pro-legalization of marijuana for any use, not just medicinal.

The Gallup polling has indicated for the first time in history that a majority of

Republican voters now support the legalization of marijuana, period, i.e. not just medicinal marijuana.

America's substantial block of voters who are fueled by the Internet and cable TV are neither Republican nor Democrat, exclusively, and when they swing, they win elections. President Trump's supposedly "impossible" path to victory is proof of this, as well as a case in point.

RULE #73

PICK A RUNNING MATE WHO WON'T HURT YOU.

After thirty years in Republican presidential politics, I can't think of any Republican vice presidential candidate who was impressive.

The first rule in selecting a Vice President is like the Hippocratic Oath—"first do no harm." That's easier said than done.

In 1960, Nixon chose the handsome but laconic Senator Henry Cabot Lodge Jr. Lodge took a two-hour nap every afternoon and rarely campaigned on weekends. Lodge also surprised his running mate by declaring that Nixon would put a Negro in the Cabinet. Nixon was forced to put out a quick statement saying all Cabinet members in a Nixon administration would be chosen on the bases of qualifications and merit, not color—lest he lose the southern states.

George Bush chose Dan Quayle for vice president for fear of being overshadowed by stronger potential candidates like Bob Dole and Jack Kemp. The VP nominee can't be "bigger" than the presidential candidate and there were few on the political scene whose policy ideas where thinner than Bushes.

Dick Cheney overshadowed George W. Bush and gave us a phony war to boot.

No vice presidential candidate has pulled in a big, electoral vote-rich state since Lyndon Johnson pulled Texas into the Kennedy column in 1960—and even then it took widespread voter fraud and the wholesale destruction of absentee ballots before a recount could be mounted.

Mike Pence helped shore up GOP's Evangelical base for Donald Trump in 2016. The vice president has a "lean and hungry look," as Shakespeare said of Macbeth.

MAKE SURE YOUR GLOVE FITS.

There was a day when no gentleman would leave the house without gloves and a hat. White or buff gloves in suede or chamois were required in fall, and pigskin and fur lined leather gloves were best for winter. Today, your use of gloves will most likely limited to the colder months.

Choose gloves too large rather than too small. A man's hand looks foolish squeezed into a tight glove.

RULE #74

PREPARE FOR WHEN THE VOTERS ARE PAYING ATTENTION.

People in politics easily lose sight of the fact that the average person has exponentially less interest in politics and political issues than the average political junkie possesses.

The distractions of everyday life, along with preoccupations like earning a living, paying bills, raising children, caring for family, and generally enjoying life in some form or another, make politics at best an intermittent feature of civic engagement and at worst a needless, fruitless annoyance which only gets worse, if ignored or left to its own devices.

Most people only begin to focus on politics, if at all, in the few weeks just before an election. Nixon noted that voters pay attention to a candidate's announcement of their candidacy, their acceptance speech at the nomination convention and their final election eve appeal . . . but little else, if anything, in between.

The longer presidential nominating system, which forces candidates to run virtually nonstop for two years, may be of endless interest to political junkies, but most of the public is only vaguely aware that the process is ongoing, and that there has been some early jousting among the candidates.

Because of this dynamic, any polling done early in an election contest is largely meaningless. In 2007, former New York Mayor Rudy Giuliani maintained a hefty lead in the polls among Republican voters. Within just a year, Giuliani had dropped to fourth place and by the end of January 2008, he was out of the race entirely.

As is the case with almost everything about his political forays, Donald Trump appears to be an exception. However, Trump's fame was so great and his name recognition so high, right from the start, that the conventional rules could not be applied as cleanly to the Donald. He had begun the race with the public already having interest in his candidacy, thanks to the many many years he had devoted to marketing himself and the Trump brand in so many other arenas.

Whatever the voter attention span may be, whatever the window of opportunity they may have to make their mark, great politicians like Jack Kennedy, Ronald Reagan, and Richard Nixon prepare meticulously for those key moments in a presidential campaign when most voters will be paying the most attention.

RULE

TRUST YOUR POLLSTER.

#75

A candidate who proceeds to run a multi-million-dollar media budget to change public opinion without sophisticated polling is a loser. A great pollster may have an ideology, but they must divorce it from his or her analysis of raw polling data. That is never to say a poll should cause a candidate to change a heartfelt position. Rather, it is a question of emphasis and deemphasis that must be examined.

This ability to divorce your ideology from your analysis, and the ability to find consensus ideological issues, both strengthening your base and attracting undecided voters, is what makes a great pollster. Doug Schoen is in this mold. A one-time liberal Democratic candidate for Congress, Schoen is a giant among pollsters because of his ability to give you a cold dispassionate reading of "the numbers."

Tony Fabrizio is another who has deep-seated conservative beliefs but when it comes to issues, he knows which fights to pick and which to avoid.

Dr. Richard Wirthlin, a Mormon and closet polygamist, was Ronald Reagan's pollster and always sugarcoated news to the Gipper. Bob Teeter, the Rockefeller-to-Bush liberal Republican pollster was very bright but risk adverse in a profession that requires risk.

Pat Caddell was the last cowboy pollster who led where the numbers dictated and first found the American thirst for reform which led to the election of Donald Trump.

A pollster can make or break a candidacy, without even appearing to do so. The subtleties can be infinite. While the process of polling may be "scientific," the distillation and interpretation of the polling data is very much an art that is grounded in skill and talent.

Who wore it better? (Photo courtesy of Stone Cold Truth.)

RULE #76

DO NOT FOOL YOUR TAILOR.

The same way you should trust your pollster, you should trust your tailor. An experienced tailor knows what you are up to. He has already cast a professional eye over your manly form; he knows that you cannot hold in your gut for more than a minute or two and that your true waist will reassert itself while he is measuring you for trousers.

STONE'S RULE #77

TROUSERS MUST HANG FROM THE WAIST.

The fluid line of a man's silhouette is the key to great tailoring. With a proper suit the lines of the suit jacket skirt and the line of the trousers should be unbroken to the eye.

Trousers should hang comfortably from the waist rather than be cinched with a belt.

That is why I prefer braces, which are called suspenders by Americans. (In Britain, suspenders are garters meant to hold up socks like Dagwood Bumstead.)

A fuller-cut trouser is often more flattering to the silhouette and may help a great tailor like Mr. Cheo, a master craftsman in New York of Chinese ancestry who trained on Savile Row.

If you must wear a belt it, must be of the highest quality leather and the buckle must be simple and nonostentatious. No Confederate flags, no sports logos, no skull and cross bones, and no "Forget Hell, the South will Rise Again artwork."

I avoid recognizable designer house logos on belt buckles, although Hermes is acceptable if you live in Southern California, the South of France, or the Italian Riviera.

KNOW IF YOU DRESS RIGHT OR DRESS LEFT.

"Where you hang your junk?" A good custom tailor will ask when he makes suit trousers. A gentleman either hangs to left or to the right, but one should know.

THE BEST CANDIDATE IS ONE WHO'S LOST ONCE.

First-time candidates, if they are smart, are much more effective in their second bid for public office. Like Lincoln, Tom Kean Sr. lost bids for Congress and the governorship in New Jersey before winning over a nine-man field in the primary and snatching the governorship of the Garden State from Congressman Jim Florio.

Running a losing effort teaches a candidate how the political system and the media work and prepare them to be a better candidate. Candidates who are afraid to lose are candy asses.

Mario Cuomo would have never become governor if he didn't have the guts to run for mayor of New York City and lose. Chuck Percy wouldn't have won election to the US Senate in 1966 if he hadn't run a losing campaign for governor of Illinois in 1964.

Andrew Cuomo wouldn't be governor of New York today if he hadn't lost his 2002 run for the governorship and been elected attorney general.

Losing sharpens a candidate's candidate skills. A candidate whose performance does not improve after losing will be a habitual loser.

A candidate who bounces back from a first-race loss and returns to the field a more skilled candidate, hungry enough to put themselves through another campaign grind, is the next best thing to an incumbent running either for reelection or for another public office.

STONE'S RULES

PART #5

HOW TO STAY ON TOP

RULE #79

THE HIGHER YOU GET ON THE FLAGPOLE, THE MORE PEOPLE CAN SEE YOUR ASS.

This is one of the maxims of the late Arlen Specter, formerly counsel for the infamous Warren Commission, staunch proponent of the "Magic Bullet" theory and longtime US Senator from Pennsylvania. I agree with his saying but not his conclusion of who killed JFK and why.

Specter was one of the great survivors of American politics. Elected district attorney of Philadelphia after bolting the Democratic Party and becoming a Republican, Specter was subsequently defeated in races for mayor, district attorney, governor, and US Senator.

In 1980, after never abandoning his commitment to public service and his dream of holding statewide office, Specter was elected to the US Senate in that year's Reagan-led Republican tidal wave and went on to serve in the Senate for thirty years.

In the US Senate, Specter was a staunch defender of civil liberties, privacy and free speech. After 9/11, Specter was one of a few who resisted the Bush administration's systematic efforts to create a police state, but Specter also sought to be smart about the war on terrorism. I slept better at night knowing Arlen Specter was in the Senate.

Specter's maxim is another way of saying that public exposure in politics cuts both ways. The more exposure you get, the greater the chance that what is exposed may not be your best face but, instead, your ass.

A POLITICAL MISTAKE IS LIKE A FART . . . SOMETIMES YOU HAVE TO JUST STEP AWAY.

Nixon once told me this, which is a blunt nugget of wisdom wrapped in a bit of toilet humor.
I think it speaks for itself.

RULE #80

LAY LOW, PLAY DUMB, KEEP MOVING.

These were the rules of life for the late Lee Atwater, my former business partner, once-Republican National Chairman, and a fellow mastermind behind George H. W. Bush's 1988 presidential campaign victory.

Atwater's sage comes from the South Carolina experience. He was a master at keeping a secret and feeding you disinformation. Atwater even considered his best friends competitors.

When he identified a true enemy in the internal infrastructure of the Reagan White House or in the Bush campaign entourage, Atwater would flawlessly execute a plan to vanquish his enemies, who would be none the wiser than that Lee was their best friend.

He rarely left fingerprints.

The Atwater life rules are crucial for a young political operative who needs to avoid arousing the jealousy or ire of the "old bulls."

ADMIT NOTHING; DENY EVERYTHING; LAUNCH COUNTERATTACK.

These are my three corollaries to Lee Atwater's "lay low, play dumb and keep moving."

Even though a warrior never goes on defense, quick denial of political charges against you must be placed on the record as part of your counter attack. Your supporters want to, and must, hear it so it is necessary to rapidly rebut any charges before ramping up a counter-offensive.

Never admit to anything. I am reminded of Joey Bishop in the movie, *Guide for the Married Man*. Caught in bed with another woman by his wife, who demanded to know "Who is that woman?" Without missing a beat, Bishop replied, "What woman?"

Some are going to say I am employing this technique in dealing with the so-called Russian collusion matter. But the stone-cold reality of it is that the giant roiling smoke cloud of fake news insinuations, implications, and loose charges of collusion between the Russians and

Donald Trump or the Trump campaign is itself, in fact, the ultimate dirty trick.

It takes an expert like me to know one when he sees one and, rest assured, the radical left and their Democrat Party mouthpieces have pulled the dirtiest trick in modern American politics with this Russia collusion hoax that they have been cynically perpetrating on the American people for nearly two years, as of this writing.

Dealing with this hoax on a daily basis only reminds me that the sooner you get off defense and on to the counterattack, the better off you will be. If you are on defense, you are losing.

At just twenty-six, John P. Sears was a political aide to former Vice President Richard Nixon. Sears's understanding of how mass media works, particularly the political press from the 1960s to the 1980s, was brilliant.

Attorney General John Mitchell drove Sears from the Nixon White House, but Sears went on to become Ronald Reagan's presidential campaign manager in both 1976 and 1980.

Sears understood that a small group of media elites would cover a campaign based on a perception of whether the campaign was progressing or not. He also knew that a campaign, particularly the front runner's, had to be proactive in making news that would generate voter interest and, thus, movement among both the voters and the reporters trying to figure out how a candidate is doing.

If a campaign is not dynamic, it is static. If a campaign is not on the move, it is floundering. Politics is kinetic. Politics is motion.

The late Arthur Finkelstein was a heavy-hitter political consultant for conservative and Republican candidates around the country from the early 1970s until the early 2010s. Art was a genius at understanding free media and how it can create the *perception of motion* that is critical to a successful political campaign.

Finkelstein was so perceptive about the electoral landscape in America that in 2004, nearly four years before Hillary Clinton's first failed presidential bid and twelve years before her second, equally disastrous presidential campaign, that Art said of Clinton, "She will put off Democrats from the center. In terms of the Republicans, Hillary Clinton is a wonderful candidate for the presidency."

Working with Finkelstein, I got a US Senate candidate in the Iowa Republican primary to call for John Wayne's birthplace in Winterset, Iowa to be made a national shrine and added to the National Register of Historic Places.

Suddenly an obscure former Lieutenant Governor running for the US Senate was on the front pages of Iowa's newspapers and being featured on all of the network affiliates in every media market in the Hawkeye state.

While politics is motion, a campaign is as much about the *perception of motion*, even where there may not be actual movement on some issue or another.

To make the news, often you must create news.

STONE'S RULE #84

HYPOCRISY IS WHAT GETS YOU.

New York Governor Eliot Spitzer's problem was not that he patronized high-priced call girls but rather that he prosecuted numerous such escort services when he was attorney general.

Spitzer called for campaign finance reform after essentially taking nine million dollars under the table in illegal campaign loans from his billionaire father.

In the end, it was hypocrisy that brought down Eliot Spitzer.

RULE

DON'T SHOOT THE GUY BEHIND YOU.

#85

In politics, the hardest position to occupy is frontrunner in a race for public office. It is incumbent on the frontrunner to make news, show progress, and, above all, appear unconcerned about the challengers nipping at their heels.

The most treacherous mistake for any frontrunner is also their greatest temptation: avoiding risk in order to maintain a lead.

Campaigns are about capturing the interest of the voters and holding that interest.

When a candidate has nothing new or specific to say, choosing to play it safe by saying little or nothing of interest, or nothing at all, voters will look elsewhere for scrappier, more vocal, more aggressive candidates who have something to say in their effort to gain ground.

If you are not gaining votes, you are losing votes.

But just as the frontrunner is expected to be the leading voice in any campaign, the frontrunner is also the central target.

As the inevitable attacks start to flow it is easier, or at least more tempting, for an already risk-averse frontrunner to counterattack the trailing candidate(s), instead of having the discipline to stay on message and continue generating interest away from, not towards, an opponent's attacks.

A candidate who attacks a trailing candidate forfeits frontrunner status by doing so, and becomes just another one of the pack, fighting to secure a public office.

The corollary to this rule would be "Don't punch down." Attacking those trailing you, or of a lesser position on the political totem, only elevates them and increases their credibility.

GREEKS BEARING GIFTS ARE PROBABLY TRYING TO FUCK YOU UP THE ASS.

When things seem too good to be true, it is because they are. People with schemes to make hundreds of millions of dollars for little effort on your part in which they get you to use your strategic mind and guile in return for equity are barking up the wrong tree.

I once helped a company selling lottery products. I had a nice share of equity. Then I learned that the founder and CEO of this company, which would require scrutiny and approval by gaming regulators across the United States, was a convicted felon who had embezzled more than one million dollars from a previous employer to pay for an opulent life style and a gambling habit.

When I presented this information to other shareholders, I was asked to leave the company and sell my shares and the CEO was given millions more in capital. The CEO couldn't get a contract with a public entity to save his life and burned through six million dollars in seed capital, staying at the finest hotels, eating at the finest restaurants, leasing a mansion in Palm Beach, and leasing luxury cars for himself and his wife.

The other shareholders were in love with his financial projections and couldn't see that they would never win a public contract with a convicted felon controlling the company.

The CEO, rather than being prosecuted, was bought out of his stock for nine million dollars. The company has yet to make a dime and the shareholders are SOL.

RULE

#87

DROP YOUR VOICE; DON'T SHOUT.

This is a rule that demented Democrat witch doctor Howard Dean should have learned. Hillary Clinton would have benefited from it, too, though Clinton's voice is so naturally shrill and grating that probably no amount of vocal modulation could ever take the edge off of that auditory knife, which would cut its way through one's brain no matter what the volume. But I digress . . .

Dropping your voice for emphasis is the best way to focus listeners on your key point. Reagan used this technique in his best speeches, although as a trained actor he knew when to bellow, "Mr. Gorbachev, tear down this wall!"

Nixon learned the technique from Roger Ailes and used it in his famous "train in the night" acceptance speech at the 1968 Republican Convention, in which he recounted his memories as a small boy listening to train whistles in the night and "dreaming of far-off places."

A masterful political orator can grip an audience with a near whisper, but any political speaker who has to shout has probably already lost the audience.

RULE

PICTURE THE PICTURE.

#88

The Internet has truly supercharged the ability of almost anyone to flash a visual image around the globe literally in a matter of seconds.

Before this ability became available to anyone with a computer and a connection to the World Wide Web, AP, and UPI had the exclusive ability to reach millions through what were called "wire photos."

Subscribers to the "wire services" would instantly and simultaneously receive anything and everything that "came over the wire," printed out on a giant continuously fed printer solely dedicated to this purpose. The system was very much a precursor to another revolutionary, but transitional, technology: the "fax" or "facsimile" machine.

Mike Deaver, who choreographed Ronald Reagan's presidency, knew the value of image as captured in a split-second snapshot that all the world would see.

Nixon understood this too. He and JFK were chatting amiably after their second debate in 1960, when an AP photographer approached. Nixon immediately began putting his finger in Kennedy's chest like he was telling him off—just as Nixon had done to Soviet Premier Nikita Khrushchev in a famous photo from the so-called "Kitchen Debate."

The AP photo of Nixon appearing to face down Kennedy ran nationwide. JFK was furious, telling Arthur Schlesinger, "That man is a shit. A total shit."

Ah, but Nixon was perceptive and quick-thinking enough to "picture the picture" that would soon be seen by millions.

Candidates for public office should not dress significantly differently than the voters dress.

When John F. Kennedy's brother-in-law Sargent Shriver hastily joined the McGovern presidential ticket when original VP nominee Tom Eagleton turned out to have been hooked up to jumper cables, he made his first campaign foray in custom designer Christian Dior French suits with high arm holes and an Continental cut and extremely expensive Gucci loafers.

Entering a working-class bar in Milwaukee to campaign, he looked like a Martian. A cheer went up when he shouted, "a round for the house" and the customers shouted for beer, then he added "and I'll have a Courvoisier," proving he was an asshole.

John Kerry's Hermes neckties, not to mention his much-aired fondness for wind-surfing along with his lifestyle of the rich and famous, put him far apart from the average voter. It didn't help that the closest Kerry ever came to dressing like a regular American was in 1971, when he donned an olive-drab fatigue jacket to disdainfully testify to the US Senate Foreign Relations Committee that American fighting soldiers in Vietnam were worse than "Jen-jis" (Genghis) Khan.

This is a Stone Rule that, more than anything, comes down to something that seems to be disproportionately lacking amongst America's permanent political class: common sense.

It also cuts both ways, with an implicit corollary rule to not dress BELOW your audience. Just as a candidate should not wear a crisp business suit and tie to a country fair, neither should that candidate show up to a gathering of business professionals in jeans and shirt-sleeves.

A candidate might have to attend numerous functions in any given day, each with a wildly different group of voters. Rushing from a business roundtable breakfast to a union hall lunch to a chicken-and-dumplings dinner at a rural volunteer fire company can make it a challenge to feel and look comfortable while dressing in a way that will also makes voters feel comfortable with a candidate.

"Costume changes" are neither possible nor desirable in the thick of back-to-back-to-back campaign stops, no matter how disparate the audiences may be. This would be an absurd waste of candidate and campaign time, and one screwup in the event advance is all it would take to leave the candidate looking like a fool entering a room in garb grossly mismatched to the gathered voters.

The solution is consistency in dress, with room for variation, from business casual to business formal. Whatever their dress, there is one thing, above all, that the candidate must maintain, at all times: dignity.

STONE'S RULE #90

ALWAYS CONTROL THE LIGHTING.

Marlene Dietrich and John F. Kennedy both understood this rule, and exploited it to their every possible advantage.

If you want to be seen in your best light, you must be seen in *THE* best light.

Never allow photographs, films, or speeches under fluorescent lights.

Fat faces should be lit from above to minimize jowls (Nixon used this one).

Know which side is your worst and never be photographed from that side.

Use backlighting when necessary. It's why you'll never find a bad photo of "Lili Marlene."

RULE

#91

DON'T BE AFRAID TO INTRODUCE PEOPLE.

After ten national Republican presidential campaigns, my Rolodex is fat with contacts—movers and shakers in all fifty states.

I know people who can help people who are friends. I never fear putting people who can help each other in touch. I don't reserve "favors" for myself and I refuse to "use the chit."

The favor bank is, and should be, unlimited.

Keeping score is stupid—unless you help someone who then refuses to help you in return, even once. Such people belong on a "special" list.

Connecting allies is never a losing proposition and though they may not see it immediately, your generosity, magnanimity, and political ubiquity will be remembered by your friends and respected by the rest.

POLITICS IS ABOUT THE FUTURE, NOT THE PAST.

Politicians and their political strategists often have a self-destructive tendency to want to fight the last war. The best strategist learns from past experiences, but always recognizes that no two campaigns are ever alike, because no two sets of election circumstances are ever alike.

Superficially, the nuts and bolts of any political campaign will appear roughly the same as every other campaign you have seen. If the rote mechanics of a campaign made any significant difference, there would be no need for a superior strategy, deft maneuvering, or the constant inventive creativity that are what transform a credible effort into a victorious campaign.

Apply the lessons of the past to realities of the battle at hand, but don't try to impose them if they don't fit the situation. What worked in the past won't necessarily work now. Politics demands innovation and reinvention because it is a constantly evolving landscape.

You have to keep the voters interested, but also perpetually refine your ability to best your competitors, who are also evolving and refining their skills with every new battle.

The voters themselves are always looking forward.

Americans are amazingly resilient and, though we are affected by the past, we are more concerned with the future and the possibilities it holds.

When the voters reject the image of you being presented to them, reinvent yourself. Bill Clinton was a master of this. So was Richard Nixon.

All through the 1950s and 1960s as both vice president and presidential candidate, Nixon signed autographs, correspondence, and all but the most formal documents as "Dick Nixon." In 1962, while running for governor, his campaign pamphlets included "Dick Nixon's Twelve Point Plan for California Progress."

1966 saw the death of "Dick" Nixon and the rise of Richard M. Nixon. Gone were Dick Nixon the Redbaiter and Dick Nixon the Partisan Slasher. Tricky Dick had disappeared and in his place was now Richard M. Nixon—seasoned, experienced, and a man who had time to reflect on the great issues of the day.

Nixon literally stopped signing his name as "Dick Nixon" and now signed his name as "Richard M. Nixon." Research into the online market for Nixon autographs would show that the dogged political phoenix's autographs ceased being "Dick Nixon" after his metamorphosis.

It was with the Richard M. Nixon persona that Nixon staged one of his many odds-defying political comebacks, winning the presidency in 1968, just eight years after losing his first bid for it, by the smallest margin in history, to Senator John F. Kennedy. Just as there was no longer a "Dick" Nixon after 1966, so too disappeared Senator "Jack" Kennedy in January of 1961.

In politics, the old aphorism about perseverance is slightly modified: if at first you don't succeed, try, try—just don't try the same thing—again.

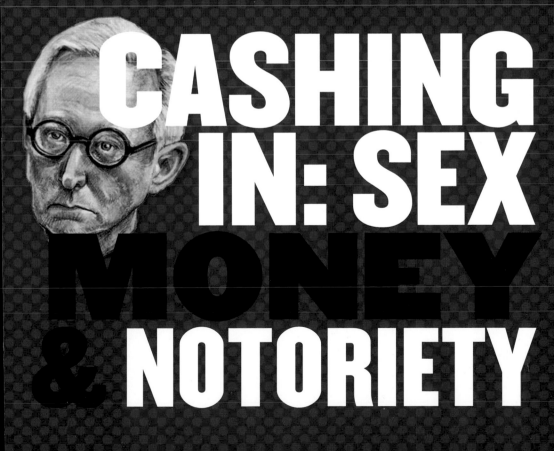

STONE'S RULES

PART #6

CASHING IN: SEX MONEY & NOTORIETY

NOTHING IS ON THE LEVEL.

Flamboyant New York attorney Roy M. Cohn, the notorious right hand man to Senator Joseph McCarthy and a Reagan confidant, told his mob godfather client Joseph "Fat Tony" Salerno that "nothing is on the level. Everything can be fixed. Just costs money."

"The US Supreme Court?" Fat Tony asked.

"Costs a few dollars more," Cohn replied.

Lawyer Roy Cohn and his mob client "Fat" Tony Salerno told me in 1979 that "Lyndon did it."

DON'T TELL ME THE CASE. TELL ME THE JUDGE.

Politics permeates everything. Only a dope would think otherwise.

Judges are public servants who may not have won an election race (elected judges are more rare in America than those appointed to the bench), but they have nonetheless succeeded in the political process.

Some judges are fair and honest; others are on the take, or taken with their own power. The absolute authority a judge unilaterally wields, from behind black robes on a high perch overlooking their fiefdom, hardly lends itself to greater humility or, frankly, humanity.

The complexity and the sheer volume of all of the laws on the books, from federal down to municipal, rather than creating precision and definition in dispensing justice, only allows greater room for judges to be arbitrary and capricious.

This is why Roy Cohn used to say, "Don't tell me the case . . . tell me the judge."

RULE #96

THERE IS ONLY ONE PARTY: THE PARTY OF GREEN.

This is the real thing that ideologues and novices fail to understand. In Washington, DC, the Republicans and Democrats at the Congressional level—even with lessened civility—still answer to the same special interests like Goldman Sachs, the House of Saud, Big Oil, Big Hollywood, Big Pharma, the hedge funds, and other robber barons.

It was California Speaker Jesse 'Big Daddy' Unruh who said, "Money is the mother's milk of politics."

In the end, money greases everything—money in campaign contributions, money financing nonprofits, money in public relations campaigns but also, most importantly, money for reelection.

Until you get the money out of politics, which, let's face it, will never happen. Unless there is quite literally free media advertising (not public financing) given to candidates, this will not change.

Whatever their party affiliation, they are all in the Party of Green, driven by the need to get the green to win another term.

MONEY IS LIKE MANURE ON A FARM—NO GOOD IF YOU DON'T SPREAD IT AROUND.

When guys grease me, I have to grease a small army of gunsels, operatives, spies, informants, lawyers, web designers, graphic artists, researchers, and the young army of people who work with me.

Young people, especially, depend on prompt full payment of their compensation so they can pay their rents/mortgages, put gas in their cars, and buy groceries. Delays in cash flow hurt these working people and can not be tolerated.

Pay your bills and pay them on time. If you order a political assassination, pay for it!

Stinginess is the worst of sins. A man who does not over-tip is a piker.

A waiter, doorman, grocery bagger, or cab driver busts their ass to make less in a day than you spend for lunch. The cost of your cigars is greater than what they make an hour.

I've worked for tips during the summers in Connecticut—not an easy way to make ends meet.

Bad tipping is a sign of a lack of true success and financial and social comfort. Even if you don't have it, tip like you do.

My friend Marvin Liebman, former communist, Israeli Terrorist, London producer, and Catholic convert, always said, "The one time you must go first class is when you're broke."

STONE'S RULE #99

NEVER PASS UP THE OPPORTUNITY TO HAVE SEX OR BE ON TELEVISION.

have lifted this from Gore Vidal, who is right on both scores.

LET'S TALK ABOUT SEX, BABY.

Sex is an intensely personal thing. Voters don't care about sex as long as it's between consensual adults. I always thought it was stupid of Republicans to try to impeach Bill Clinton over an Oval Office blow job when they could have impeached him for selling nuclear secrets to the Chinese.

I have always been a libertine and have never made any bones about it. I find it amusing when left-wing websites accuse me of being in league with the religious right in promoting their agenda in the 1980s. Nothing could be further from the truth. Once asked by a reporter about my own sexuality, I said I was a "try sexual—I've tried everything." Trust me, I got more than my share during the "Summer of Love."

I have long said and written that the Evangelical Christian insistence on opposition to gay marriage and legal abortion would destroy the Republican Party by costing us any chance with younger voters.

Even when it's bad, it's still pretty good.

Good pizza is the slice you can find at 3:00 am when you are smashed or high after a night of revelry. Beyond that, pizza is a very personal thing.

The style of pizza in my native Connecticut is a thin, coal oven charred pie with sausage or their garlicky white clam pizza. The people in Chicago like a deep-dish pizza that is mostly bread.

I once caught Frank Morano, a New York radio personality and political activist, ordering this deep-dish style pie from a joint near his radio station, which almost got him banished from his native Staten Island once it was learned—Staten Island being a citadel of great pizza.

A thin, well-charred Neapolitan pizza is the ideal breakfast with a triple espresso as far as I am concerned. Generally speaking, however, you should always avoid any pizzeria called "Ray's" or "Ray's Original." Also avoid pizza places called "John's," with the exception of

"John's of Bleeker Street" in the West Village. This is a shrine to great pizza.

When I was growing up in industrial Norwalk, Connecticut, a short bicycle ride from where I lived was a full-service Italian restaurant owned by a retired prize fighter named Phil Baker. A lightweight whose real name was Philip J. Matro, Baker turned out a phenomenal pizza topped with fennel-laced Italian sausage.

The distinct aroma and wonderfully-unique taste of Phil Baker's pizza pies sticks with me to this day. When the State of Connecticut decided to finish construction on Route 7, the restaurant was razed to make way for progress.

I spent the rest of my life looking for any pizza that could match this boyhood ideal.

SIZE *DOES* MATTER.

It still amazes me when I see commercial or political graphics in which the key message is not printed boldly and in the largest possible type size. Voters observe political information in little more than a quick scan.

According to David Ogilvy, the legendary advertising genius, billboards (which I disdain) need no more than six words to be effective.

Size also matters in the *boudoir*—don't let anyone tell you differently. Guys who brag about their "oral technique" have small dicks.

RULE

NEVER RIDE IN A WHITE LIMOUSINE.

#103

Limousines themselves should be off limits for candidates seeking public office. This is not to be confused with the limousine service that comes with being elected governor, president, or to the leadership of Congress. Those are the perks of office and should be used in the governmental capacity.

I once worked for a Republican candidate for attorney general of Virginia who showed up at a GOP rally in a vintage Rolls-Royce limo that belonged to a wealthy Republican supporter. The AP wire photo made the front page of a daily newspaper the next day, whereupon his opponent branded him "the Rolls-Royce Candidate of the Wealthy."

White limousines are particularly gauche; their use should be limited to strip clubs and pimps.

ETHNIC TRAITS ARE WHAT THEY ARE.

Whoever said you should speak German to your dog, French to your horse, Italian to your priest, Spanish to your mistress, and English to your wife, almost had it right.

The Italians have a style that is sometimes impractical; there is nothing more beautiful than the lines of a classic Alfa Romeo or a 1960s vintage Ferrari, but neither is likely to start on a reliable basis.

The real trade-off in life is figuring out how to balance form and function. I'm sure that a boxy, cookie-cutter Lexus sedan is as reliable as the day is long, but I will never drive anything so nondescript and generic.

When I lived and worked in Washington, DC, I drove a 1972 Citroën DS-21 Pallas (sedan) and a 1970 Citroën DS Familiale Break (the station wagon model). I switched to Jaguars in the late 1970s when parts and service for the Citroen's became scarce.

Jaguars had a reputation for both beauty and unreliability, but this is only true of Jaguars made before Ford Motor Company acquired the British car maker in 2000. Jaguars remain stylish and sexy.

Yes, if you have an older model it might break down. But you'll still look good next to it waiting for roadside service.

1972 Citroen DS-21 Pallas. My car in Washington. (WIkimedia Commons).

RULE #105

BE BLASÉ IN THE FACE OF CELEBRITY.

People who gush when they meet, or are in the presence of, a celebrity show their weakness, lack of sophistication, and lack of social status. On top of this, it is just really uncool.

One must be blasé, even vaguely detached and indifferent, to the fact that you are in the presence of a superstar.

When I met Madonna at a South Beach cocktail party in the early 1990s, I asked her what she did for a living.

Large, ostentatious cufflinks are for New Jersey mafia dons, Las Vegas lounge singers, and Harlem pimps (if there are any left). Cufflinks should be understated, small, and elegant. Enamel, gold, or silver are fine but never large and brassy, and big stones of any kind verboten.

No coffee grinders, no giant gold coins, no jet planes, and no faux gems.

Buy a pair of black and a pair of blue silk knots. Put them in the ticket pocket of your suits when traveling. They go with everything and can sub for a missing cufflink in a pinch.

STONE'S RULE #107

CUFF LENGTH UP TO YOU—BUT SHOW SOME.

A gentleman needs to "show linen" at the end of the sleeve of a well-cut suit or sports jacket. How much you show is up to you. I recommend at least an inch and a half for Americans. For myself, I prefer the English and Italian style of two inches.

This is just as true with button cuffs as it is with turn-back cuffs (which the uneducated call French cuffs, although no one can find any particular connection to those garlic-smelling frogs).

STONE'S RULE #108

TWO-INCH CUFFS.

The American norm in one and a half inches.

Two inches make you look taller and weight the cuff, so it hangs properly. Look at a photo of Prince Philip in a suit made for him by his long-time tailor, Poole of London.

That's what a gentlemen's trouser should look like. Two-inch cuffs.

The notion of marking your possessions with an artful logo of your initials was a popular style in the 1920s and 1930s. A gentleman had his initials painted on his Louis Vuitton luggage and, discreetly, on the driver's door of his Packard convertible cruiser.

Today monograms are a bit trickier. Put them on the cuff of a button-down shirt and you mark yourself a salesman from Toledo. Monograms are for shirtfronts only, exactly one inch below the left nipple. Breast shirt pockets are a mistake, unless you are a nerd. A dress shirt is pocketless. The monogram should be small, discreet, and understated.

AVOID EXCESS.

An excess of jewelry should always be avoided, but the gentlman may wear gold or silver cufflinks and a watch-chain, if he favors a pocketwatch. He may also wear a flower in his buttonhole, for this is one of the few allowable devices by which he may brighten up his attire without being garish.

RULE #110

A WORD ABOUT JEWELRY: DON'T.

This is an area where less is more. Necklaces or chains are for South Philly guidos. ID bracelets are for the outer boroughs. Keep it minimal.

A tasteful family crest ring is fine—make a crest up like Trump did if you don't have one. A wedding ring if you're hitched and a slim tasteful watch that does not weigh three pounds is also OK.

I have some woven bracelets from my granddaughters. I love these and wear them daily.

THE BROOKS BROTHERS-STYLE WHITE, ALL-COTTON, BUTTON-DOWN COLLAR SHIRT IS AN INDISPENSABLE ELEMENT OF EVERY GENTLEMAN'S WARDROBE.

Bill Buckley wore his with a black bow tie and cummerbund with a tuxedo. Gianni Agnelli fastened his wristwatch over the cuff of his and never buttoned the collar down.

Looks great with sleeves rolled up with a ribbon belt and khakis. Goes with every conceivable color and pattern of sports coat or suit (except double-breasted).

In pink or light blue with a madras jacket, it's perfect for summer. Paired with a herringbone sports jacket and a black knit tie, it's perfect for fall and winter.

These days the best one is made by Kamakura, a Japanese company. After changing hands and factories so many times, venerable old Brooks Brothers has lost the proper "roll" of the collar. Kamakura has it—and the price is right.

Throw a folded one in your travel bag—it goes with everything.

TOO MUCH OF A GOOD THING IS ABOUT RIGHT.

Donald Trump's election victory shows, among many other things, that media have become so diverse that there is no such thing as overexposure.

In any election campaign, especially a national race, name recognition is a basic and often expensive goal. Trump's years of marketing himself made that irrelevant in his presidential bid.

His taste it not mine—except Mar-a-Lago, his Palm Beach club/mansion, which he restored meticulously to it 1920s grandeur using a team of the finest artisans.

You can find the Trump name on games, coffee mugs, T-shirts, bottled water, vodka, cologne, men's suits, and extra-large condoms, and they all sell. He is a marketing genius. What other Manhattan real estate mogul was an internationally known figure? Zeckendorf?

There is only one, and now he is the President of the United States. That is not luck, my friends. That is drive, determination and pure *genius*. Period.

WHEN YOUR CANDIDATE TELLS YOU YOUR TV SPOT IS ON TOO HEAVILY AND PEOPLE ARE COMPLAINING ABOUT SEEING IT TOO MUCH—YOU ARE JUST STARTING TO PERMEATE THE PUBLIC CONSCIOUSNESS.

Media have come a long way from the day we had three major networks and some powerful local independent TV stations. Then viewers were limited to the thirteen channels on the dial—some of those channels had snow because not enough programming was available or operating a channel would not be economically feasible. A small broadcast monopoly existed.

Today, when media are diverse—with hundreds of cable news networks, talk radio, blogs, websites, radio stations and broad use of the Internet—it takes focused and expensive repetitive efforts to punch through an idea to the voters in an atmosphere where they are constantly bombarded with a cornucopia of information.

To punch through a message in this din, put up one kickass TV spot and pile up the repetitions, being careful to place time on the proper cable news networks to reach conservatives, women, Democrats, older men, and other target voter groups that your polling tells you are susceptible to your message.

This takes repetition and discipline to load up enough GRPs behind the spot to punch through.

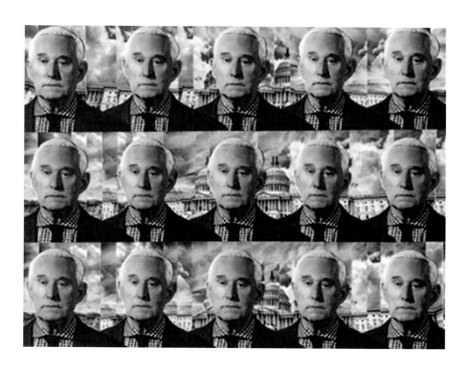

STONE'S RULES

PART #7

ROGER'S RULES FOR SURVIVAL

STONE'S RULE #114

"COCK YOUR HAT. ANGLES ARE ATTITUDES."

Frank Sinatra nailed this one.

It's about the angle of your Homberg. It's about the knot in your silk Italian scarf. It's about the right shoes with the right stove-pipe leg jeans. It's about your pocket square of a paisley silk and a white linen monogrammed handkerchief you carry at all times, folded in a pocket. It's about the piece of thread that a Savile Row tailor sews into the back of the button hole in your lapel in order to hold the stem of a flower of boutonniere just so. It's about the ticket pocket on the jacket, the two-inch waist band on the full cut reverse pleated trouser with two-inch cuffs. It's about black silk knotted cufflinks which work in a pinch with everything. It's about carefully tying your formal bow tie ever slightly imperfectly, so everyone will know you actually tied it yourself. It's about knowing what you look good in and wearing it. It's about developing a uniform in which you know you look your best but also recognizing that to break the rules you must first know what the rules are and prove to be the exception to them. Above all your clothing must have attitude that tells people who you are.

RULE

#115

DICK NIXON'S SILVER BULLETS

Dick Nixon made a mean martini and was quite proud of his martini-mixing skills, calling them "Silver Bullets." Gin was the old man's preference, over vodka.

Undoubtedly Nixon honed his mixology skills tending bar at "Nick's Hamburger Stand," an impromptu canteen put together by the enterprising Navy lieutenant for war-weary service members passing through Nixon's post in the South Pacific in World War II. Dick served up booze and burgers. Nixon served at Guadalcanal and later at Green Island as officer in charge of the South Pacific Combat Air Transport Command, supervising C-47 cargo operations. Lieutenant Commander Nixon was legendary for his ability to acquire "hooch" for the boys.

Generally speaking, Nixon was not introspective. He hated to talk about the past, always looking forward instead. It was hard to get him to talk about Ike, McCarthy, JFK, LBJ, and the deep secrets he held close for so many decades. But after two drinks the old man became absolutely loquacious and would reveal astonishing things, cloaked in Nixonian intrigue, of course.

"More than one of these and you want to beat your wife," Nixon reportedly told his then-26-year-old assistant John P. Sears.

The coolest thing about Nixon's "Silver Bullet" was that it was borrowed by Nixon from no less a legend than British Prime Minister and wartime leader Winston Churchill.

DICK NIXON'S SILVER BULLET MARTINI RECIPE.

The Recipe

Ingredients
- One (1) bottle of small to medium sized green olives with pimento
- Dry Vermouth of choice
- Fine Russian vodka (or Tanqueray gin, as Nixon preferred)

Assembly
- Drain the brine from the bottle of olives, leaving olives intact
- Refill olive bottle with water; shake vigorously; drain water completely
- Refill olive bottle with dry Vermouth; refrigerate the bottle
- Chill a traditional martini glass
- Fill a cocktail shaker with ice, preferably a vintage Tiffany hammered silver art deco shaker
- Fill the shaker with vodka (or gin, according to preference) until the ice is covered
- Shake VERY vigorously—if there are not tiny shards of ice floating on the

surface of the Silver Bullet, you have not shaken the mixture vigorously enough

- Pour the mixture into the chilled martini glass
- Add one Vermouth-drenched olive from the jar
- Return the Vermouth olive jar to the refrigerator for use with your next Silver Bullet

RULE #117

IT'S GRAVY, NOT SAUCE.

I grew up in the Connecticut suburbs of New York City in a working-class family that's half-Italian. Every Sunday, my mother would rise early to assemble her "Sunday Gravy," which is what Italian Americans in Philadelphia, much of New Jersey and enclaves of Connecticut called your basic red sauce. The recipe is precise and the specific list of ingredients inviolable, or the entire production is doomed from the start.

The centerpiece ingredients of this Italian American staple are canned imported San Marzano tomatoes. San Marzano is not a brand of tomato, but rather a type of plum tomato from a specific region of Italy. No other canned imported tomatoes will do. Be vigilant about tomatoes labeled "San Marzano Style" tomatoes because such an annotation on the can means someone is selling you *fugazi*. I repeat: only real San Marzano tomatoes will do.

Now, to the recipe . . . first, take a medium-size yellow onion and dice it.

Sauté the onion on a medium flame in olive oil specifically labeled "For Sautéing & Grilling" until translucent.

Take three large cloves of minced garlic and add to the pan. Note: garlic has a lower burning point than onions and should only be added when the onions are translucent, but before they brown. Be careful not to burn the garlic.

Add two cans of whole San Marzano plum tomatoes, including the juice. Using a spatula, crush and break apart the tomatoes.

Add two-and-a-half tablespoons of oregano, one tablespoon of mixed Italian spices (basil, marjoram, thyme, rosemary, sage). Add coarse black pepper and salt to taste. Remember the tomatoes are naturally salty, so be cautious.

Let this mixture cook at a low to medium heat, as it will need to thicken. Add one can of imported tomato paste and an equal size can of water. Continue cooking. The flavors only meld after several hours cooking at a low heat, being careful not to burn the gravy nor to allow it to become too thick.

There you have it: Sunday Gravy. If you want to employ it in a hearty meat sauce, I prefer a mix of equal parts ground beef, ground veal, and ground pork, sautéed with the onions but *before* you add the garlic—AGAIN, BE CAREFUL NOT TO BURN THE GARLIC.

Best served over rigatoni, ziti, penne, or a thin #11 spaghetti. *Mangia*!

Buy quality garments and take good care of them and they will serve you well. This includes rotating your suits allowing them to air out between wearings. Avoid dry cleaning because the chemicals used in that harsh process will stress fibers that are already weakened from absorbing black blue or gray dye. This is why suits that have been repeatedly dry cleaned begin to shine. It is better to dip a whisk broom in cool water to clean a suit, allowing it to dry by hanging it outdoors but not in direct sunlight.

To keep trousers sharply creased, a gentleman pulls the pant leg towards him before sitting down. In dire circumstances, a pair of trousers can be put between a pair of bed mattresses to restore their crease.

A proper pair of braces, known in the United States as suspenders, allow your trousers to hang from the waist so as not to cinch your silhouette the way a belt would. Under no circumstances are elastic suspenders that clip on the waist-band of your trousers with a metal clip acceptable. This is also true of pocket protectors.

THE PRESS IS NOT THE ENEMY.

This Stone Rule may come as a surprise, given the contentious and even hostile relationship that exists between the "mainstream media" and most successful self-made, independent-minded political activists and leaders.

Richard Nixon hated the press even though the print media made him a national figure with the Alger Hiss case in 1947. Nixon also leaked with such skill as vice president to Ike that he enjoyed great ink from the *New York Herald Tribune*, *Los Angeles Times*, and the *New York Times*.

Nixon was 100 percent right about the press corps' favoring JFK in 1960. He also got pretty rough treatment from the California media during his aborted 1962 comeback bid, running for governor of that state.

Jim Doyle, who was spokesman for Watergate Special Prosecutor Archibald Cox and later a crack political reporter for *Newsweek*, taught me to understand and respect the power of people who buy ink by the barrel—or get 100,000 hits a day, to translate this into the parlance of the Internet age.

Be straight with, and helpful to, reporters and most—but certainly not all—will be straight with you, and maybe even honest, too.

Those who are not straight or honest with you are to be fed either disinformation or nothing at all, whatever is needed to make them look foolish. *Capisce?*

I first advocated a Trump candidacy for president in 1988. Donald wasn't interested . . . yet. (Photo courtesy of Nydia Stone.)

Dog bites man is not a story.
To break through the media clutter of the modern-day world your ideas have to be pungent, over-the-top, provocative, and outrageous.

Politics is theater but sometimes it is performance art, for its own sake.

THEY ARE ALL PINK ON THE INSIDE.

I hate racism. I abhor discrimination. And as a conservative, I have a deep belief in the civil rights of every person, regardless of color.

Richard Nixon had an unblemished record on civil rights. In 1956, as vice president, Nixon went to Harlem to declare, "America can't afford the cost of segregation." The following year, he played a key role in rounding up the votes that ensured passage of the Civil Rights Act of 1957 in the US Senate, winning the praise of Dr. Martin Luther King.

Nixon supported the 1964 Civil Rights Act and although he employed a southern strategy to win the votes of whites through his "tough on crime" and "win the war in Vietnam" campaign themes, he also desegregated the public schools and instituted "affirmative action" programs to redress historical discrimination.

During Richard Nixon's presidency, the Department of Justice budget for civil rights enforcement was increased by 800 percent. Nixon appointed more black Americans to federal offices than JFK and LBJ combined.

The Nixon administration created the Office of Minority Business Enterprise. Under Nixon, SBA loans to minorities soared by 1,000 percent and aid to black colleges doubled.

When Nixon became president, fewer than 18 percent of public schools in the south had been desegregated. At the time Nixon was driven from office in 1974, that number had reached 89 percent.

There were no race riots, no harsh rhetoric, no demonstrations, and no violence. Attorney General John Mitchell carried out the mandate from the Supreme Court to desegregate the schools in an orderly and firm—but calm—manner.

A Republican who is not a strong advocate of civil rights is of no interest to me. We are the party of Lincoln and must be foursquare in support of equal justice for all people.

Attorney General and Nixon political advisor John Mitchell told me he directed the White House's 1970 illegal, dark money Townhouse operation to put hundreds of thousands of dollars of laundered money into George Bush's 1970 presidential campaign. It was called the "dress rehearsal for Watergate." (Wikimedia Commons)

THE DEMOCRATS ARE THE PARTY OF SLAVERY; THE REPUBLICANS ARE THE PARTY OF FREEDOM.

Southern Democrats of the old Confederacy were the progenitors and defenders of slavery, all the way through the Civil War, and continued to propagate institutional racism for another century with "Jim Crow" segregation laws, and similarly racist public policies.

Consistent with its horrible racist history, today's Democrat Party seeks to keep black people in bondage, slave to the Democrats' insidious and destructive public policies that intentionally construct an artificial social and economic hierarchy around elitist welfare state paternalism. Just like the Democrats of yesteryear, today's Democrats want black Americans securely confined to the Democrats' narrow, exploitive political plantation.

What I think black Americans want, and deserve as much as any American, is a piece of the economic pie—a real stake in the game and the ability to rise on their talent and merit, rather than be perpetual supplicants of the state.

They want to be employers, not just employees.

The job of government in all this is the opposite of what Democrats have been pushing for nearly a century, with their "progressive" big government scams and schemes. Rather than controlling the world with endless regulations and restrictions and mandates, the government's role must be to remove barriers to free enterprise.

Government must foster programs that get free enterprise capitalism moving in our inner cities, as well as in any part of America that is suffering chronic economic depression. Donald Trump understood this, intuitively. It was a huge factor in his victory. Now President Trump must deliver on this.

Sadly, most Republicans don't put forward such a message or propose policies consistent with it, despite its being their political "birthright," as the party of Lincoln.

It is up to the Republican Party to wake up and shake off its largely reactive sleepiness about the question of race in America. It does not require embracing racial identity politics to give full-throated thoughtful attractive voice to the better alternative to the Democrat Party's cynical racialist opportunism and systematic political predation on minority groups.

STONE'S RULE #123

MANY ARE COLD, BUT FEW ARE FROZEN.

This was the political maxim a small-time political operative from New Jersey named Arthur Miller. Arthur was 340 pounds and had a truly terrible toupee, but he had a confident strut and his organizational and persuasive talents were remarkable.

Miller also controlled the young Republicans in New Jersey as part of his faction of the New Jersey State Republican Party. He was true wheeler-and-dealer, always looking to "wet his beak," as legendary political boss George Washington Plunkitt would say.

Arthur never viewed today's adversary as tomorrow's enemy. He believed anyone in politics could be persuaded to do something, once you convinced them it was in their best interest. "Many are cold, but few are frozen," Miller would say.

The key is to separate the cold from the frozen, and find out what will turn the cold opponent into a warm ally . . .

SIZE MATTERS.

Senator John Tower of Texas was diminutive but impeccably tailored in custom suits by Anderson and Sheppard of Savile Row, London. Short in stature and a US Senator from Texas, Tower was the only man who could justify a custom English tailored suit and highly polished black cowboy boots.

Congressman J. J. "Jake" Pickle was an LBJ crony and Congressman from Texas. Pickle weighed three hundred pounds and was known for his slovenly dress and ill-fitting baggy poplin suits from Sears Roebuck.

Tower admonished Pickle one day about the merits of English tailoring and recommended it to Pickle. "That's a nice suit you got on John, what does it cost in a man's size?"

THE FAT SHOULD AVOID HORIZONTAL STRIPES. THE THIN SHOULD AVOID VERTICALS.

Horizontal stripes make you look broader and shorter. Vertical stripes make you look taller and thinner.

Dress with each in accordance to your weight and body type not your preference.

The horizontal striped shirt that Cary Grant wears in *To Catch a Thief* looks great on him but would look terrible on Sydney Greenstreet or any other 350-pounder.

MEN OVER THIRTY-FIVE REQUIRE PLEATS IN THEIR TROUSERS UNLESS VERY FAT.

The major trouble with trousers in modern times is their lack of material. Trousers today are like the little church in the valley—no ballroom.

Lyndon Johnson once told the President of Farrah Slacks who was making him several pairs of complementary trousers that he didn't want to feel like "a fella straddling a wire fence." This is why English tailors and their Italian cousins invented full-cut pleated trousers with many variations including reverse pleats.

A good tailor can use pleats to trim a stout gentleman down or make a thin gentleman look broader, always thinking of the silhouette he is creating.

The only place pleats don't belong is on blue jeans.

As G. K. Chesterton said, you can search all the parks in all the cities and find no statues of committees. Advertising pioneer David Ogilvy was also fond of this saying.

The essence of effective leadership and success in the political arena most often requires decision-making authority to rest in the hands of a single person. You travel fastest alone. You risk no leaks when only you have the information.

Decision-making by committee is a sure way to lose a bid for public office or to blow the launch of a commercial advertising campaign. When products like a television commercial or a sophisticated voter mailing are tweaked by twenty people, there are simply too many cooks in the kitchen. Committees breed timidity and interpersonal accommodation rather than pointed results. The thrust of important political arguments and buzz words get diluted when they pass through many hands for revision.

Central authority is required for quick decision-making and blitzkrieg is sometimes required in the political or business arena. Leaving key or pressing decisions in the hands of a committee is death. I won't work for any campaign or corporate client where final decision-making authority isn't vested in one person.

"War councils breed defeat," said General Douglas MacArthur.

STONE'S RULE #128

MAKE YOUR MOST DIFFICULT PHONE CALL FIRST.

I learned this from South Carolina political legend and one of the longest serving US Senators in history, Strom Thurmond.

Thurmond was as aggressive a user of the telephone as any politician could be. Strom would call cronies, college and military chums, farmers, business owners, local pols, county sheriffs, judges . . . really anyone who had any influence with South Carolina voters.

Thurmond would comb the newspapers to find people whose children had died or the names of the wives of recently deceased veterans. He'd call the parents or the widow or the next of kin and express his heartfelt condolences. Everyone got a card from the good Senator on their birthday, too.

In these "keeping in touch phone calls," Strom would dole out federal goodies as prolifically as he would home-spun advice. I once walked in on him when he was giving a widow in Florence the precise recipe for a concoction of prune juice and lemons that Strom told her would cure both her cold and her constipation.

This endless stream of personal phone calls to back home was Thurmond's folksy way of helping his constituents, but also of keeping their vote.

"Make your toughest phone call—the one where you must deliver bad news—early in the day, or it will never get made," Ol' Strom told me.

STONE'S **RULE** #129

THE BIGGER THE SCORE, THE LONGER THE GESTATION.

America is a great country because a person either born here or who comes here with nothing can achieve the American Dream.

I have gotten great satisfaction out of political battles I have fought and the entrepreneurial endeavors in which I have made money.

A business deal that could yield potentially enormous amounts of money will never happen quickly. The more moving parts a deal has and the less simplicity, the longer it will take.

True entrepreneurialism requires patience to achieve great wealth.

THREE MEN CAN KEEP A SECRET OF ONE, IF TWO OF THEM ARE DEAD.

This ominous maxim was posted on the wall of the Louisiana mob boss Carlos Marcello's headquarters. He means nothing is a secret if more than one person knows about it. In truth, there are no secrets. If you tell someone something assume it will leak—even if what you tell them is said in jest.

In this case, two men *can* keep a secret. (Wikimedia Commons)

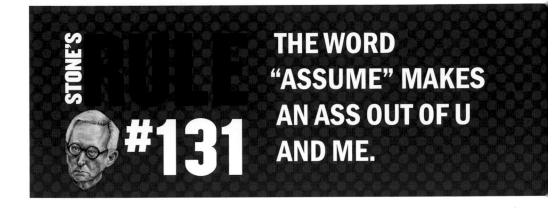

THE WORD "ASSUME" MAKES AN ASS OUT OF U AND ME.

It's a common saying, but this anecdote proves it's always worth remembering:

Jeb Stuart Magruder, Director of the Committee for the Re-Election of the President (CREEP) was a pretty boy who the old Nixon hands like Nick Ruwe and Ron Walker routinely derided as "Steve Stunning."

In 1972, Magruder was my supervisor, as was his right-hand man Herbert L. "Bart" Porter. Both went to jail for their role in the Watergate coverup.

Magruder was an insufferable jerk. Nevertheless, it was Porter who dressed me down in front of Magruder in a staff meeting when I said, "I assume . . . ," in one of my answers to a question from my boss.

"Assume!?" Porter screamed. "Look at the letters—it makes an ASS of U and ME."

I felt like an insect, but Porter was right.

Never assume. KNOW.

A WAY TO KEEP YOUR TROUSERS PRESSED.

Use your bed as a trouser press. A very good plan is to place the trousers under the mattress of a bed, as the pressure will mimic that of trouser-stretchers, helping them from becoming baggy at the knees.

The clip-on bow tie is always to be avoided. The pre-tie bow tie can be acceptable, but a gentleman should know how to tie his own. Perfection is actually to be avoided. The properly tied bow tie should be slightly askew.

These day most gentleman will wear a bow tie only for formal wear. Yet a properly sized bow tie, jauntily knotted, can work for some men. Think Daniel Patrick Moynihan, Arthur Schlesinger Jr., George Will, and at one time, Tucker Carlson. It is worth noting that many people associate bow ties with salesman and carnie barkers. Therefore, it would be safe to say that there are certain professions say, trial attorney, where a bow tie is probably not the best choice.

The following method is the simplest way to tie a bow tie: Put the tie round your neck with the left-hand end about a couple of inches below the right. Tie in a single knot and bring the left-hand end (which should still be the longer of the two) over so that it covers the right.

Make the left-hand loop of the bow with the right-hand end, which should then be at right angles to the left. Then bring the left-hand up so that it goes right round the left-hand loop. Then fold the left-hand end and push it through the center loop which has been formed. If this is done properly, the left-hand end makes the right-hand bow of the tie, and all that remains to be done is to pull the under part of the two bows tightly and the tie will be fixed.

WHITE DRESS SHIRTS AFTER SIX.

This is an old custom. White is the most formal shirt a man can wear. Broad stripes, thin stripes, subtle plaids, and more business-oriented colors are for daytime. At night, a true gentlemen dining at the '21 Club" or Gallagher's Steak House on 52nd and Broadway should have changed into a clean white shirt for his evening affairs. Going up to Harlem to listen to jazz and do the club scene inappropriately shirted would be in a sartorial error.

A compromise: white collar and cuffs with a striped solid or tiny patterned dress shirt can sub for those who think all white is too boring.

STONE'S **RULE** **#135**

BLUE BLAZERS AND KHAKI PANTS ARE GREAT FOR COLLEGE STUDENTS OR SATURDAYS, BUT NOT APPROPRIATE FOR BUSINESS ATTIRE.

In 1980, I recommended Lee Atwater to Ronald Reagan's national political director, Charlie Black, to handle the Southern Region of the Country for the Reagan campaign.

Atwater had managed Strom Thurmond's tough reelection in 1978 and had been an ally and fellow blues enthusiast who I kept in touch with. Atwater went on to obliterate former Texas governor John Connally in the South Carolina Republican Presidential Primary.

It was in the same primary that Atwater and I went to Bill Buckley's dissolute brother, Reid, Buckley who was living off of scotch and public speaking gigs. The brother sounded identical. I induced Reid Buckley to tape radio commercials attacking George Bush and then dubbed on a lead-in that said, "Well Mr. Buckley, what do you think about George Bush?" They were killer.

I told Atwater that he could not come to Washington without a suit, so he agreed to go to Brooks Brothers with me to pick out a couple of suitable models for his new job. Atwater blanched when he saw the price: $275. I was spending $1,800 on custom made suits at the time.

RULE #136

COWBOY HATS ARE LIKE HEMORRHOIDS—EVENTUALLY EVERY ASSHOLE GETS THEM.

Cowboy hats are fine if you're from Texas or Nevada or Wyoming or Montana. I find the people who wear them in SoHo or Tribeca or Beverly Hills or Santa Monica or San Francisco are uniformly assholes.

No one who wasn't born in a western state should be allowed to wear a cowboy hat. Although, I guess I would grant an exemption for rock stars, but even there, it is distasteful. I respect it on the range but not in the fashionable boites in Manhattan.

After Lyndon Johnson selected Hubert Humphrey as his running mate, he forced Humphrey to go to his LBJ ranch and dress in an identical cowboy hats and western garb as Johnson did. Humphrey looked like a mini-me. Johnson did it to humiliate him and to show him who would be boss in the new Johnson administration.

RULE #137

NEVER WEAR A DOUBLE-BREASTED SUIT AND A BUTTON-DOWN COLLAR.

The peak lapel double breasted suit is the most formal of suits.

The button-down shirt is the most informal of shirts. They don't go together. A double-breasted suit requires a starched collar, either Windsor, spread or medium, or long-point.

Under no circumstances should a button-down collar shirt be worn with a double-breasted suit.

I know. Fred Astaire did it. You're not Fred Astaire.

DARK RAINCOATS ARE FOR HOODLUMS.

A raincoat is a necessity if you live in a part of the country or the world with precipitation. Nothing beats the classic Burberry Trench coat in various weights and linings.

Failing that, raincoats should be light in color and utilitarian in their ability to repel rain water.

Dark raincoats are low class and for hoodlums, Mafioso, or Chinese gang members.

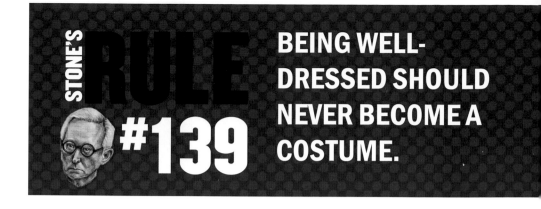
Being well turned down should never morph into a costume. I like the way Tom Wolfe dresses. I once snagged a seat next to him at a *Spectator* dinner party. His tailoring is fine. But his look is too outdated for everyday wear by anyone but him. No one makes celluloid collars anymore. His look is Victorian. It works for him, but it would not work for anyone else.

Classic men's styling has really not changed since the 1930s and a well-cut, double-breasted suit works work as well in 1938 as it does in 2018. Men's style may have taken some detours, like the shapeless sack suit taking over in the '50s and the polyester Deco inspired men's wear of the 1970s, being the decade that good taste forgot. Yet men's style today has rotated back to the fundamentals of the 1930s.

Tucker Carlson reportedly abandoned the bow tie because he correctly determined that it had become costume. And he is at least partially right. Even though

I like a nattily tied bow tie, I would not wear them out of fear for exclusivity. I feared that in this sartorial transition by Tucker would rob him of his mojo. Fortunately, that has not happened largely because of his unerring good taste in the selection of four-in-hand neckwear. Tucker has not only survived without his bow ties—he has thrived. This dude can rock the regimental stripes.

STONE'S RULE #140

HE WHO LAUGHS LAST LAUGHS HEARTIEST.

"Revenge is a dish that tastes best when eaten cold," said George L. Clark Jr., Chairman of the Kings County (Brooklyn) Republican County Organization. Clark, whose mother was Italian, was paraphrasing an important Sicilian proverb.

I will often wait years to take my revenge, hiding in the tall grass, my stiletto at the ready, waiting patiently until you think I have forgotten or forgiven a past slight and then, when you least expect it, I will spring from the underbrush and plunge a dagger up under your ribcage.

So if you have fucked me, even if it was years ago, don't think yourself safe.

STONE'S RULES

I. Entering the Arena

#1 There Are Men of Action, and Men of Words.

#2 You Can't Win If You Don't Get in the Game.

#3 Don't Hide Your Scars, They Make You Who You Are . . .
     But Don't Fight the Last War, Either.

#4 Past Is *Fucking* Prologue.

#5 Make Your Luck.

#6 Reach Higher.

#7 Miracles Do Happen.

#8 If Life is a Performance, Be a Costume.
     + Develop Good Dressing Habits Early.

#9 Dress with *Sprezzatura*.

#10 Dress British, Think Yiddish.

#11 To Win, You Must Do Everything.

#12 Think Big. Be Big.

#13 Never Quit.

#14 Never Be Scared of Anyone or Anything.

II. First Impressions

#15 If You Are Engaged in Any Business or Profession, You Are
     Much More Likely to Succeed If You Are Well-Dressed Than
     if You Are Badly Dressed.

#16 The Only Thing Worse in Politics Than Being Wrong Is Being
     Boring.

#17 Look Good. Feel Great.
+ Solid Sartorial Advice.

#18 White Shirt + Tan Face = Confidence.

#19 Great Leaders Have Personal Style.
+ Being Well Dressed Doesn't Take Time.

#20 Use a Cigar.

#21 Great Leaders are Detached.

#22 Build a Foundation for Your Wardrobe.
+ Cheap Underwear is Even a Greater Mistake with Men than with Women.

#23 The Blazer Is the Foundation of a Gentleman's Wardrobe.
+ No Bolo Ties East of the Mississippi.

#24 The Suit.
+ Avoid Dry Cleaning.

#25 A Black Square-Bottomed Knitted Silk Knit Tie Is a Necessity.

#26 Build a Foundation for Your Wardrobe.

#27 The Cut of the Suit Matters.
+ Remember the Silhouette.

#28 Never Hold a Meeting Unless You Know What Result You Want Out of the Meeting.

#29 Be on Time.

#30 Important Meeting? Blue Suit.
+ Your Pants Have To Fit.

#31 Mix and Match.
+ Grey Flannel, Brown Suede Shoes, Yes!

#32 Two-toned Shoes and White Bucks Only After Memorial Day.

#33 A Black Suit Should Only Be Worn By Chauffeurs or Undertakers.

#34 Tuxedos With Notched Lapels are for Waiters.

#35 Hang a Name on Your Opponent.

#36 Brown Is the Color of Shit.

#37 To See How a Candidate Will Perform in Office, Look at Their Campaign.

#63 Pay Your Political Debts.

#64 Campaign Finance Reform Has Done for Politics What Pantyhose Has Done for Finger Fucking.

#65 Use the Internet to Do with Thousands of Dollars What Once Required Millions.

#66 Never Turn Down a Major Party Nomination.

#67 What's in the Public Domain is Fair Game.

#68 A Tan Makes a Man Look Vigorous and a Deep Tan Makes a Man Look Prosperous.

#69 Everything is Recycled.

#70 Move to the Right for the Primary, Move to the Center for the General.

#71 Politics Is the Art of Addition, Not Subtraction.

#72 Folks Want to Get Government out of the Boardroom and the Bedroom.

#73 Pick a Running Mate Who Won't Hurt You.
  + Make Sure the Glove Fits.

#74 Prepare for When the Voters are Paying Attention.

#75 Trust Your Pollster.

#76 Do Not Fool Your Tailor.

#77 Trousers Must Hang from the Waist.
  + Know If You Dress Right or Dress Left.

#78 The Best Candidate Is One Who's Lost Once.

V. How to Stay on Top

#79 The Higher You Get on the Flagpole, the More People Can See Your Ass.
  + A Political Mistake Is Like a Fart . . . Sometimes You Have to Just Step Away.

#80 Lay Low, Play Dumb, Keep Moving.

#81 Admit Nothing; Deny Everything; Launch Counterattack.

#82 Politics Is Motion.

#83 Politics Is the Perception of Motion.

#84 Hypocrisy Is What Gets You.

#85 Don't Shoot the Guy Behind You.

#86 Greeks Bearing Gifts are Probably Trying to Fuck You Up the Ass.

#87 Drop Your Voice; Don't Shout.

#88 Picture the Picture.

#89 Don't Dress Above the Voters.

#90 Always Control the Lighting.

#91 Don't Be Afraid to Introduce People.

#92 Politics Is about the Future, Not the Past.

#93 Reinvent Yourself.

VI. Cashing in: Sex, Money, & Notoriety

#94 Nothing is on the Level.

#95 Don't Tell Me the Case. Tell Me the Judge.

#96 There Is Only One Party: The Party of Green.

#97 Money Is like Manure on a Farm—No Good If You Don't Spread it Around.

#98 Over-Tip.

#99 Never Pass Up the Opportunity to Have Sex or Be on Television.

#100 Let's Talk About Sex, Baby.

#101 Pizza is Like Sex.

#102 Size *Does* Matter.

#103 Never Ride in a White Limousine.

#104 Ethnic Traits are What They are.

#105 Be Blasé in the Face of Celebrity.

#106 Cufflinks Should Be Understated, Small, and Elegant.

#107 Cuff Length Up to You—But Show Some.

#108 Two Inch Cuffs.

#109 Monograms.
   + Avoid Excess.

#110 A Word About Jewelry: Don't.

#111 The Brooks Brothers-Style White, All-Cotton, Button-Down Collar Shirt is an Indispensable Element of Every Gentleman's Wardrobe.

#112 Too Much of a Good Thing Is About Right.

#113 When Your Candidate Tells You Your TV Spot Is on Too Heavily and People are Complaining about Seeing It Too Much—You Are Just Starting to Permeate the Public Consciousness.

VII. Roger's Rules For Survival

#114 "Cock Your Hat. Angles are Attitudes."

#115 Dick Nixon's Silver Bullets.

#116 Dick Nixon's Silver Bullet Martini Recipe.

#117 It's Gravy, Not Sauce.

#118 Never Wear the Same Suit Two Days in a Row.

#119 The Press is Not the Enemy.

#120 Avoid the Obvious.

#121 They Are All Pink on the Inside.

#122 The Democrats are the Party of Slavery; the Republicans Are the Party of Freedom.

#123 Many Are Cold, but Few Are Frozen.

#124 Size Matters.

#125 The Fat Should Avoid Horizontal Stripes. The Thin Should Avoid Verticals.

#126 Men Over Thirty-Five Require Pleats In Their Trousers Unless Very Fat.

#127 No One Ever Built a Statue to a Committee.

#128 Make Your Most Difficult Phone Call First.

#129 The Bigger the Score, the Longer the Gestation.

#130 Three Men Can Keep a Secret of One, If Two Of Them Are Dead.

#131 The Word "Assume" Makes an ASS Out of U and ME.

#132 A Way To Keep Your Trousers Pressed.

#133 Tie Your Own Bow Tie.

#134 White Dress Shirts After Six.

#135 Blue Blazer and Khaki Pants are Great for College Students or Saturdays, But Not Appropriate for Business Attire.

#136 Cowboy Hats are Like Hemorrhoids—Eventually Every Asshole Gets Them.

#137 Never Wear a Double-Breasted Suit and a Button-Down Collar.

#138 Dark Raincoats are for Hoodlums.

#139 Being Well-Dress Should Never Become a Costume.

#140 He Who Laughs Last Laughs Heartiest.